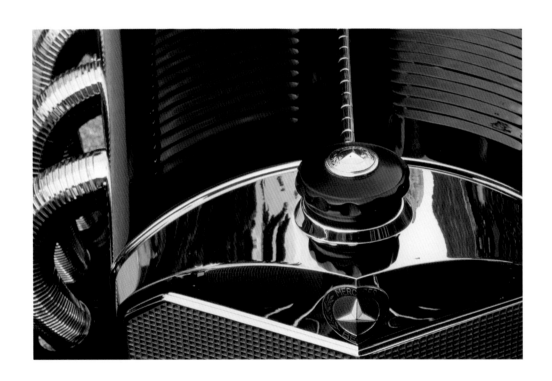

MERCEDES-BENZ
SILVER STAR CENTURY

DENNIS ADLER   FOREWORD BY STIRLING MOSS

MBI Publishing Company

> Thus the Mercedes Comes, O she comes, This astonishing device, This amazing Mercedes With Speed
> —WILLIAM ERNEST HENLEY, *A SONG OF SPEED*

DEDICATION

For Jeanne, the star in my life.
To Maryalice Ritzmann, Dr. Josef Ernst,
Ute Baumann, and the wonderful people at
DaimlerChrysler Classic, without whose help and generous
contributions this book could not have been possible.

First published in 2001 by MBI Publishing Company,
729 Prospect Avenue, PO Box 1, Osceola, WI 54020-0001USA

MBI Publishing Company books are also available at discounts in bulk quantity for industrial or sales-promotional use. For details write to Special Sales Manager at Motorbooks International Wholesalers & Distributors, 729 Prospect Avenue, PO Box 1, Osceola WI, 54020 USA.

Library of Congress Cataloging-in-Publication Data Available

ISBN 0-7603-0949-3

On the front cover: A trio of magnificent Mercedes cars. From top to bottom are a 1930 710 SS bodied by the English firm of Forrest-Lycett, a 1955 300SLR that was Rudolf Uhlenhaut's personal car, and a 2001 SLK.

On the frontispiece: The hood and external exhaust pipes of a 1930 Mercedes-Benz SSK once owned by Count Carlo Felice Trossi. *Ralph Lauren Collection*

On the title page: A 1956 Mercedes-Benz 300Sc bodied by Pinin Farina. It is the second of three Mercedes-Benz 300 models created by Pinin Farina.

On the back cover: A quartet of Mercedes models, including a 1902 40-horsepower roadster, Clark Gable's 1957 300Sc Cabriolet, Ralph Lauren's 1955 300SL, and a 1971 280SE 3.5 Coupe.

On the endpaper: Benz production in 1894 included the Patent Motorwagen Vis-à-vis, shown here with Carl Benz (in light suit) and his family. *DaimlerChrysler Classic*

Edited by Keith Mathiowetz
Designed by Katie Sonmor

Printed in China

Contents

Foreword

By Sir Stirling Moss

It is a privilege to have been asked to preface Dennis Adler's work on Mercedes-Benz, since the company played such a profound role in shaping not only my career as a professional racing driver, but also indirectly through the people I worked with there—so much of my personal life.

It may seem an odd thing to recall, but what first impressed me so hugely about the company's approach, methods, and general philosophy was actually a bowl of warm water, soap, a face-flannel, and a dry towel. I'll explain why shortly.

Even as a small boy I had heard much about the magic of Mercedes-Benz, the Three-Pointed Star, and their racing team's crushing dominance of top-level Grand Prix racing. Whenever Mercedes had gone racing, they had in some way set the pace. During their absences from the racing circuits of the world—enforced either by politics, the aftermath of war or economic recession—their rivals had enjoyed making hay while the sun shone, because they must always have had a sense that—if and when Mercedes might return—their all-round commitment and staggering technical competence would again prove absolutely indomitable!

Of course, the record books told us that their cars had won the 1908 French Grand Prix, and then again in 1914, and how through the 1930s their Grand Prix cars had simply crushed virtually all opposition. After World War II, they came back to racing in 1952, making their presence unforgettable with the 300 SL's championship season, and then in the midsummer of 1954, they unleashed their very latest Formula 1 cars in the French Grand Prix at Reims—and immediately left the rest of us gasping in their wake, while team drivers Fangio and Kling immediately finished first and second.

I was driving my own Maserati at that time. I did well enough to become part of the Maserati factory team, and on occasion we ran those new Mercedes cars close, but we always knew that it would take the most enormous slice of luck for us ever to beat them.

I was in New York on November 22, 1954, when I was told that Mercedes had offered me a test drive in preparation for the 1955 season. It was such a fantastic opportunity I couldn't sleep that night just thinking about it. One word in my diary says it all—"Wow!"

Dad and I flew to Cologne, Germany, where I was met and taken to *Hockenheim* racetrack to try one of their new 2-1/2-liter desmodromic-valved Formula 1 cars for the first time. On the damp track there I eventually equaled Karl Kling's lap record. I was very impressed with the straight-eight engine, though not so much with the car itself, which seemed rather hefty. But it also gave the impression it would be totally unbreakable. It was, after all, a Mercedes-Benz, and I was eager to be part of that operation. And then what really impressed me was that, as I clambered out of the car, rummaging in my pockets for a handkerchief or rag to wipe the oil haze and road film off my face, an impeccably overalled mechanic suddenly appeared, bearing hot water, soap, a face-flannel, and a towel!

Out there, in the middle of the desolate *Hockenheimring*, was this forethought I could scarcely credit. I thought then that to be associated with such an efficient organization, one capable of thinking of *everything*, could not be half bad.

They offered me the opportunity to drive in the same team as double-World Champion Juan Fangio, and I was not about to say no. So they engaged me to drive for them in both Formula 1 and sports car competition, but left me free to drive elsewhere whenever commitments did not clash. With Fangio as my team leader, I knew I might not be able to win the championship just yet—but whatever else might happen, I should certainly be able to learn from the great man.

I can only describe driving for Mercedes-Benz as my all-round master class in life. I learned very quickly that while Juan was a truly great racing driver, he was an even greater man. In fact, he proved to be one of several personalities that I met and worked with during

Stirling Moss and codriver Denis Jenkinson with the 300 SLR at the start of the 1955 Mille Miglia. *DaimlerChrysler Classic*

that memorable season that became enormously influential to me.

I learned at the feet of Fangio, the absolute master in my view. He was the most impressive of men, not only fantastic behind the wheel of a Grand Prix car, but stupendously successful, yet faultlessly modest, tremendously determined and competitive, yet remarkably gentle and understanding. Despite all his achievements—absolutely the standard-setter of this era in Grand Prix racing—he always remained accessible to everybody. Prince or pauper, he treated literally everybody exactly the same—with grace, and charm, and open affability . . . and I hope some of that rubbed off on me.

While I learned in his wheel-tracks for much of that 1955 season in Formula 1, I came to believe I had his measure in sports cars, and while always a tough competitor he seemed to acknowledge this, and there was never, ever, a cross word between us.

I also enormously respected and liked Mercedes' famous team manager, Alfred Neubauer. While his public image was loud, tough, and authoritarian, to us, he was immensely warm, endearing, and often tremendous fun. While one moment he could rap out orders like a sergeant major, he was also capable of great sensitivity and understanding, and in relaxed moments could have us all rolling with laughter.

My first race for Mercedes was in Argentina, and in those days the long flight to Buenos Aires in a piston-engined DC6 was incredibly tedious and boring. Sensing that his young drivers needed a moment's levity, Neubauer suddenly began roaring from the back of the plane *"Der Moss, der Herrmann, kommt hier!"*

The twin toilet doors on that airliner were cramped together in a kind of vee-shaped lobby. Neubauer—with his huge roly-poly figure—was pretending to be stuck between the toilet doors. That was typical.

And then there was engineer Rudi Uhlenhaut, perhaps my closest contact of all within the Mercedes team. He was not only a wonderful engineer, he was also a naturally talented driver, capable of lapping almost as quickly as we, his drivers. He spoke perfect English, and the rapport and understanding, which grew between us, were enormously fruitful.

I have to say there was nothing easy about driving the world's finest racing cars that year. In the W 196, my feet were splayed wide apart, with a massive clutch housing between my shins, two pedals to the right, the clutch pedal way to the left. The car rode very comfortably but everything about it felt heavy. The gearchange was difficult because it was an unconventional layout, and although the cars were always very strong, and very fast, they were quite difficult to drive in the wet, and prone to weaving under power, wet or dry. The W 196 always demanded—and was given—immense respect. I won my first Grand Prix, my home event at Aintree circuit, Liverpool, in one of the "Silver Arrows," and at Monza, in the Italian GP, I vividly remember settling into my rhythm behind Fangio in our streamliners, when his car flung up a stone, which smashed my aero screen. I found myself drowning in the airstream, so I had to make a pit stop to see if anything could be done. To my astonishment (I should have known better), the team had a replacement available, which the mechanics whipped onto the car and sent me away again in 36 seconds! Next time out, if the screen were broken, I just had to press a button and a standby would pop up in its place—without needing to make a pit stop. *That* was Mercedes-Benz.

This kind of peerless attention to detail, and readiness to preempt problems, gave me perhaps my most satisfying early drives in any factory team sports car, behind the wheel of the immortal 300 SLR. In those cars we contested only six races during 1955, won five of them. We only failed to win the sixth—Le Mans—after the company board ordered us to withdraw in the aftermath of Pierre Levegh's tragic crash, which claimed not only his life but that of more than 80 spectators. The decision had come eight hours after the fatal collision. A telegram was delivered to Neubauer at the pits. The telegram was from Fritz Nallinger in Untertürkheim: "The pride of designers and drivers must bow to the grief suffered by countless French families in this appalling disaster." As a token of Mercedes' respect, the remaining two cars were withdrawn. At the time, we were running first and third.

My debut in the 300 SLR had been the Mille Miglia—the toughest sports car race on the calendar—1,000 grueling miles over public roads round Italy. For this race, I was navigated by my journalist friend Denis Jenkinson, whom I knew before I had signed up with Mercedes-Benz, but whom I got to know so much better during our Mille Miglia experience. "Jenks" had been motorcycle sidecar World Champion passenger with Eric Oliver in 1949. He combined utter fearlessness with a very quick, penetratingly clear, analytical mind, and he'd condensed the critical points of that

1,000-mile course into a hand-written paper roller of route notes, 15 feet 6 inches long.

We perfected hand signals for him to keep me advised, regardless of the noise, of hazards—or lack of them—round the next blind corner or over the next blind brow. We compiled and perfected this system during the most comprehensive reconnaissance test and preparation period I would ever experience for any race.

Mercedes' investment in its 1955 Mille Miglia program was typical of its approach, not only to competition but any objective upon which the board might set their mind. Regardless of cost, they were entirely engineering led, and it showed. It was an absolute privilege to have been part of it. The commitment Mercedes-Benz has made to engineering excellence, to forethought, to preparation throughout the last century, whether building a sports car, a grand prix race car, or a luxurious touring car, has never wavered.

Author and Mercedes-Benz historian Dennis Adler has written and photographed some of the finest automotive books published, and this latest effort, commemorating the 100th anniversary of the Mercedes brand name in 2001, is a welcome addition that will surely find its place on the bookshelves of Mercedes-Benz enthusiasts the world over.

—*Stirling Moss*

After winning the 1955 Mille Miglia, Moss (second from right) celebrates with Jenkinson, Mercedes-Benz engineering director Rudolf Uhlenhaut (second from left), chief engineer Ludwig Krause (left), and development engineer Hans Scherenberg. *DaimlerChrysler Classic*

Preface and Acknowledgments

Author Dennis Adler with the ultimate Gullwing, the 300 SLR built in 1955 for Mercedes-Benz director of engineering Rudolf Uhlenhaut.

I f I were to call this book a labor of love it would be somewhat of an understatement. My personal relationship with Mercedes-Benz goes back almost 20 years, more than 15 of which I have spent as senior contributing editor to *The Star*, the official publication of the Mercedes-Benz Club of America. Over those years I built lasting friendships with many of the people who guide Mercedes-Benz, both in the United States and in Germany. Those friendships have afforded me the privilege of writing this historic book to commemorate the centennial celebration of the first motorcar to bear the Mercedes name.

That event occurred in 1901 and launched what Paul Meyan, president of the Automobile Club of France, described as "*l'ere Mercedes*," The Mercedes Era. The car did, in all respects, establish the standards by which all other automobiles would be judged for the better part of the 1900s. And in the decades to follow, the cars of Daimler Motoren Gesellschaft would continue to raise the standard with improvements in engineering, design, and performance.

Following the merger of Daimler Motoren Gesellschaft with Benz und Cie. in 1926, there emerged from this amalgamation the greatest name in automotive history, Mercedes-Benz. Since the patent for the first Motorwagen was granted to Karl Benz in 1886, these two legendary names, Mercedes and Benz, have given the world a whirlwind ride down countless roads, from the rough macadam paved streets of Europe in the early twentieth century to the high-banked curves of the Nürburgring racing circuit. Through the grueling mountain roads of the Mille Miglia, over the vastness of the Carrera PanAmericana, and on highways and back roads the world over, the Silver Star has left its indelible mark for 115 years.

This is a history far too vast to fully cover in detail within a single volume. As such, the written history has been condensed, told in archival black and white and in new color photography, visiting the most important moments and lingering perhaps on a few that changed the course of automotive design or left us all in amazement, at a time when something amazing was least expected from Mercedes-Benz.

Gottlieb Daimler had a motto, "*The best or nothing,*" a difficult ideology to live by, but we have tried to do justice both to the man and the cars that still bear his signature to this day. As with any historical undertaking, there are those who have preceded us down the path. Mercedes-Benz history has been well documented and we acknowledge the works of many authors and historians who have published books and articles on this subject. Most notably, *Mercedes-Benz, The Supercharged 8-Cylinder Cars of the 1930s* by Jan Melin, Nordbok International Co-Editions AB, Gothenburg, Sweden, 1985; *The Star and The Laurel* by Beverly Rae Kimes, Mercedes-Benz of North America, Montvale, New Jersey, 1986; *Mercedes-Benz Personenwagen 1886–1986* by Werner Oswald, Motorbuch Verlag, Stuttgart, 1986; *Mercedes-Benz 300 SL Art & Color Edition* by Jürgen Lewandowski, Südwest Verlag GmbH & Co. KG, Munich, Germany, 1988; *Mercedes-Benz Illustrated Buyer's Guide* by Frank Barrett, MBI Publishing Company, 1998; *Fantastic Mercedes-Benz Automobiles* by Peter Vann, MBI Publishing Company, 1995; *Mercedes-Benz, The First Hundred Years* by Richard M. Langworth, Publications International, Ltd., Skokie, Illinois, 1984; and my own previous works, *Mercedes-Benz 300 SL,* MBI Publishing Company, 1994; and *Mercedes-Benz—110 Years of Excellence,* MBI Publishing Company, 1995.

In the production of this book we have had the cooperation of so many Mercedes-Benz owners that the list of those who contributed of their time and efforts would take pages. I would, however, like to express my personal thanks to my good friend and associate Frank Barrett, publisher and editor of *The Star,* official publication of the Mercedes-Benz Club of America; Beverly Rae Kimes, without whose efforts Mercedes-Benz history would be less than complete; Ralph Lauren; Paul Russell; Bud Lyon; Jerry J. Moore; Bruce Meyer; Scott Grundfor; Otis Chandler; Arturo Keller; B. Scott Isquick, and the magnificent Nethercutt Collection in Sylmar, California.

We have been blessed with the help of many friends at DaimlerChrysler including Gerhard Heidbrink, Harry Niemann, and DaimlerChrysler Classic director Max-Gerrett von Pein. A special note of thanks is also due to Dr. Josef Ernst and Ute Baumann of DaimlerChrysler Classic for their tireless efforts on my behalf, organizing an extensive two week photo shoot in Stuttgart of exceptional motorcars from the Mercedes-Benz Museum and Classic Center, supervising the construction of a photo studio, scouting locales for photography, and providing me with access to the Mercedes-Benz photographic archives, the finest repository of historical images in the world. This is a level of cooperation and preparation so characteristic of Mercedes-Benz that it serves to further underscore the company's historic commitment to doing everything possible to ensure success in any endeavor it undertakes; to live up to Gottlieb Daimler's motto.

The unprecedented help I have received from Mercedes-Benz is perhaps my variation of Stirling Moss' bowl of warm water, soap, face-flannel, and dry towel. To everyone at DaimlerChrysler Classic, I offer my sincerest and most humble thanks.

—*Dennis Adler*

CHAPTER ONE

Mr. Benz and Mr. Daimler

Before the Turn of the Century

They never really knew each other. The two greatest men in German automotive history, Gottlieb Daimler and Karl Benz, never met face to face. In fact, in the early 1880s they were barely aware of one another's work, though the distance separating the two was less than 100 kilometers, less than an hour's drive today. By 1900, Daimler Motoren Gesellschaft in Stuttgart-Cannstatt and Benz & Cie. in Mannheim had evolved into two of the most prominent automakers in the world, and at the turn of the century were well aware of each other's achievements. Unfortunately, Gottlieb Daimler passed away in March 1900 and never had the

On January 29, 1886, Karl Benz was granted German Patent Number 37435 for his invention—the Benz Patent-Motorwagen—recognized today as the first automobile. Had he waited just a little longer, Benz would have had to share that distinction with Gottlieb Daimler.

In the town of Cannstatt, Daimler had received a patent for an internal combustion engine, and with his protégé Wilhelm Maybach, began construction on a four-wheeled horseless carriage. The Daimler Motorenwagen was introduced at virtually the same time as the Benz three-wheeler. Pictured is the Daimler greenhouse workshop behind his villa in Cannstatt. In 1940 it was turned into a museum displaying Daimler and Maybach's earliest work.

opportunity to meet Karl Benz, who would live to see the two companies become one in 1926.

It's a bit of a coin toss as to whether Benz or Daimler first had the idea for a motorized vehicle. Each had taken a different course, Benz constructing his engine and affixing it to a three-wheeler in 1885, Daimler and his colleague Wilhelm Maybach, focusing more on the construction of internal combustion engines for a variety of purposes: motorwagens, lorries, public transit, motorboats, and motor-powered dirigibles—thus the foundation of Daimler's three-pointed star for land, air, and sea.

Daimler and Maybach had been partners for over 25 years before the founding of Daimler-Motoren-Gesellschaft in November 1890. Their relationship dated back to 1865,when Daimler first met Maybach as a young craftsman in Reutlingen near Stuttgart. As of 1872 they had worked together at Gasmotorenfabrik Deutz near Cologne. Here, Daimler as Technical

Director and Maybach as his chief technical engineer developed Nickolaus Otto's four-stroke engine. Ultimately Daimler found himself in dispute with Nikolaus Otto and Eugen Langen, Deutz's founders, over his improved designs, most of which had been done under Daimler's signature by Maybach. In 1882 both men resigned from the firm, going into business for themselves, and setting up shop in the small greenhouse behind Daimler's home in Cannstatt. This is, of course, skipping over the trials and tribulations of many years at Deutz and the bitter conflicts that raged between Otto and Daimler. That, and the temperament of Gottlieb Daimler himself, which led to his forced resignation in 1882. Maybach was more or less obliged to follow suit, as he later wrote, believing that he, not just Daimler, had been disgraced. One can only imagine what the future of the automobile might have been had Maybach stayed on in Cologne.

After leaving the Deutz Werk, the two proceeded to develop and patent the world's first fast-running internal combustion engine in 1883. Comparing his new engine to that of the earlier Nikolaus Otto design, Daimler said it was like a rifle to a blunderbuss. The Otto engines weighed as much as 750 pounds and operated at a mere 180 rpm. The Daimler four-stroke design was less than 100 pounds and could operate at speeds of up to 650 rpm. Two years later, Daimler and Maybach put the single cylinder, four-stroke gas engine into practice powering a motor-driven cycle or *Reitwagen*, which more closely resembled a primitive motorcycle than a motor carriage. It was, nevertheless, the first practical, motorized personal conveyance ever built. Daimler's 14-year old son, Adolf, was the test driver, taking the wooden-wheeled contraption from Cannstatt to Untertürkheim and back, a total of roughly 6 kilometers. The significance of this event, notes DaimlerChrysler CEO Jürgen E. Schrempp, makes Gottlieb Daimler deserving of the "pole position" in the history of the twentieth century.

Gottlieb Daimler had been well compensated for his work at Deutz. He bought a magnificent home in Cannstatt, and had sufficient funds to start development of the lightweight, high-speed engine. Eight years into the fruition of the project, in 1890, Max Duttenhofer, commercial privy counselor and managing director of the Köln-Rottweiler powder factory, and Duttenhofer's business associate Wilhelm Lorenz, assisted Daimler with the financial backing to establish DMG.

Karl Benz, on the other hand, rarely had enough money to pursue his business interests, and while manufacturing stationary engines in Mannheim, was developing his motorwagen on a shoestring budget, perhaps one reason he held such disdain for making design changes.

Daimler's story begins in the small greenhouse-workshop behind his villa in Cannstatt, where the 1885 motor bicycle was built, and progresses quickly to a 1.5-horsepower, four-wheel motorized coach assembled the following year. Daimler and Maybach were testing their engines in a variety of vehicles, including the first motorboat, in 1886. Karl Benz, having completed his first prototype single-cylinder three-wheeler, was busy applying for a patent, thereby making him the first to stake a claim for the design of a gasoline-powered motorwagen. German Patent Number 37435 was assigned to Benz on January 29, 1886. Had he waited just a little longer, Benz would have run headlong into Daimler and Maybach at the patent office.

Still in the developmental stages, Benz was hesitant to begin production of the motorwagen, and his testing had been confined to local roads and the yard surrounding his workshop. Benz's first attempt to drive the 1885 prototype had ended in a collision with the workshop wall! Benz had successfully tested the Motorwagen in July 1886, but it was his wife, Bertha, who would go down in history as the first woman motorist. In August 1888 she decided to drive the third prototype Motorwagen from Mannheim to Pforzheim, a distance of more than 50 miles. With her two sons, Eugen and Richard, she set out at dawn and made the trip in a single day. She wired her husband, who had no inkling that his wife and sons were off on such an adventure, that they had arrived without any significant incidents. At her suggestion, Benz made a few additional improvements to the design, including a low gear for hills. (Bertha and the boys had had to push the car up steep grades on their first trip.) By year's end, the improved third Benz motorwagen was on the road, but not the road to success.

The horse and buggy were not about to be so easily pushed aside. First of all, there were no gas stations! Motor fuel (benzene) had to be purchased at a pharmacy, and usually in small quantities, rarely more than 5 liters. Thus the world was slow to warm to the Benz Motorwagen, and it wasn't until 1892 that any significant sales were recorded. But Karl Benz soldiered on, introducing the Viktoria model in 1893, and one year

later his third design, the Velo. If there was a race to see who would build the first production motorcar in Germany, it was Benz who won with the Velo.

The path for the new model had been paved by the limited manufacture of three-wheelers built in the late 1880s, most of which were sold in Paris, France, through Benz & Co. sales agent Emile Roger. According to factory records 69 vehicles were produced between 1886 and 1893. The Mannheim works also claimed the honor of building Germany's first commercial bus in 1895. In nearby Cannstatt, Daimler and Maybach went from experimentation and development, into production introducing the world's first general purpose truck, or lorry, in 1896, a handful of four-wheel motorwagens, and the first motor driven fire engines. In 1888 they experimented with the first dirigible, and had established a taxi line in Stuttgart. Daimler now had licensing agreements in France with Panhard & Levassor and Peugeot; in Great Britain with Daimler Motor Company, Ltd. of Coventry; and in Austria with a subsidiary, Austro-Daimler, in Vienna. DMG had also become one of the first manufacturers of powerboats. In fact, in the early 1890s, Daimler's motorboats often outsold the motorcars, particularly in the United States, where they were being marketed, along with Daimler stationary engines, through an arrangement with New York piano maker and industrialist William Steinway. Although Daimler had discussed the subject of selling motorwagens as well, during a lengthy visit to the United States in 1893, Steinway was hesitant to offer them, explaining that unlike Europe, America had no established highways, and

Daimler and Maybach were not as interested in producing horseless carriages as they were in manufacturing the internal combustion engine in all its permutations, on land, on the sea, and in the air—origin of the now famous three-pointed star. By the time Daimler Motoren-Gesellschaft was formed in November 1890, Daimler and Maybach were producing motor launches and fire engines, and had experimented with a lighter-than-air craft. *DaimlerChrysler Classic*

NEXT PAGE:
The Benz Ideal Vis-à-vis was added to the Benz & Co. model line in 1898. It was a contemporary design that placed the driver in the back seat facing the passengers, hence the name Vis-à-vis, face-to-face. The new model was powered by a 1,045-cc single-cylinder, 3-horsepower engine mounted under the rear bench seat. Built atop a sectional steel frame, the Ideal had a short, 61.5-inch wheelbase. Still very carriage-like in design, it used solid axles and leaf springs. Sadly, the Ideal was obsolete the day it was introduced, as were all Benz motorwagens of similar design, following Daimler's introduction of the front-engine Phoenix in 1897.

By the 1890s both Benz and Daimler had successful businesses manufacturing stationary gasoline engines for industrial use, motorboats, fire trucks, motorwagens, and commercial vehicles.
DaimlerChrysler Classic

the roads carved out of dirt from city to city were totally unsuitable for Daimler's motorized carriages. Ironically, the Steinway Company would later import and then build and market the short-lived American Mercedes, from 1905 to 1907.[1]

As the turn of the century approached, Benz & Co. had produced over 2,000 motorcars, along with commercial chassis and delivery trucks and had various models on the road in England, France, Germany, America, South Africa, Singapore, and New South Wales. Benz also had a thriving business producing stationary gasoline engines for industrial uses and by 1899 had become the most successful automaker in the world. Thus, Benz and Daimler appeared to be moving forward at an even pace, if not always in the same direction, but this was an illusion.

By virtue of an obstinate nature, Karl Benz had become his own worst enemy, failing to regard his early

On display at the Mercedes-Benz Museum in Stuttgart, the 1897 Daimler Phoenix redefined motorwagen design at the close of the nineteenth century by placing the engine in front. A similar approach was taken in France by Panhard, which manufactured Daimler engines under license. By comparison, Benz models such as the luxurious 1899 Mylord Coupé, were still far closer to carriages than motorcars.

designs merely as stepping stones; this was the same error Henry Ford would make decades later by refusing to replace the Model T until the car was rendered virtually obsolete by his competitors. What Benz needed most was to invent the rearview mirror, so he could see how close Daimler was to running him off the road. The boldest step Benz made prior to 1900 had been the introduction of the Velo, a smaller version of the Viktoria with half the horsepower, what history might consider the world's first compact car. It was, for the time, an outstanding success. At least 1,200 were sold between 1894 and 1901. In 1898, Benz added the luxurious Ideal Vis-à-Vis, a contemporary design that placed the driver in the rear seat facing the passengers. Powered by a single-cylinder engine developing 3 horsepower at 700

LEFT:
Karl Benz and Gottlieb Daimler in later years. Daimler was born on March 17, 1834 and died on March 6, 1900 at the age of 65. Benz lived a very long life. Born Karl Friedrich Benz on November 25, 1844 he lived to see the merger of the two companies in 1926, and died three years later on April 4, at age 84.
DaimlerChrysler Classic

Wilhelm Maybach is often considered the hyphen in Daimler-Benz, having been at Gottlieb Daimler's side throughout the company's founding years, and instrumental in the creation of the 1901 Mercedes. Maybach was born in February 1846 and lived to see Benz and Daimler become one. He passed away the same year as Karl Benz and was buried near his lifelong friend, Gottlieb Daimler.
DaimlerChrysler Classic

rpm, the Ideal was anything but. A later version increased engine stroke, boosting output to 4.5 horsepower at 960 rpm, providing a top speed of around 22 miles per hour. The newest Benz models still resembled horse-drawn carriages without the horse, had their single-cylinder engines mounted in the rear beneath the seat, and for all of their virtues were obsolete the day they were built!

Daimler and Maybach had always been secretive about their designs and as the nineteenth century came to an end, the true heirs were about to stride upon the stage, and Karl Benz was about to realize that his greatest weakness was in failing to recognize their achievements. From his perspective, however, Benz had seen little reason to make sweeping changes. His motorwagens were reliable, proven designs, sales were brisk, and his stationary engine business was booming. Daimler and Maybach, however, had made a quantum leap in the late 1890s, developing and patenting a vee-twin engine. This was followed by a four-cylinder engine, a four-speed gearbox with gated linkage, a jet-type carburetor (still the basis for modern carburetors), and their first motorcar with the engine mounted in front—the 1897 Phoenix. While a bit ungainly in appearance, the Phoenix was a significant step beyond the hackneyed styling of the Benz motor carriages.[2]

That concept was Gottlieb Daimler's legacy. Troubled by a serious heart condition throughout his later years, he passed away on March 6, 1900, at the age of 65. He had been, as one close associate, Frederick Simms, the founder of Daimler Motor Company in England, eulogized him, "unquestionably the father of modern automobilism."

Following Daimler's death, the direction of DMG would be steered anew, in a roundabout way, by a customer, Emil Jellinek, a wealthy, tempestuous, Austrian merchant with a passion for fast motorcars—a passion that in 1901 would change the course of Daimler-Motoren-Gesellschaft and ignite a new era in the history of the automobile.

CHAPTER TWO

1901—The Era of Mercedes

Mr. Jellinek, Your Car Is Ready . . .

Emil Jellinek was a successful Austrian businessman (although he was born in Leipzig, Germany) who had made his fortune as a merchant in Vienna and in later years been appointed the honorary Austrian Vice-Council General in Monaco. In the 1890s Jellinek slipped into private life at his villa in Nice, and it was there, comfortably ensconced on the Cote d'Azure among Europe's wealthiest families, that he stumbled into a new career as an automotive entrepreneur.

This 1902 Mercedes-Simplex 40-horsepower is similar to the design of the 1901 model delivered to Jellinek for Nice Week in March 1901. The model pictured is regarded as oldest existing Mercedes motorcar in the world. It has since been re-restored and painted dark blue and is now on exhibit at the Mercedes-Benz museum in Stuttgart. The 1901 and 1902 models introduced many innovations, including the honeycomb radiator, 4-speed transmission, water-cooled rear brakes, and for the era, the 40-horsepower motor was one of the most powerful in the world.

21

Emil Jellinek, the renowned businessman and Daimler distributor, was something of a visionary. He saw the need for faster, more stylish cars than Daimler was producing. *DaimlerChrysler Classic*

To persuade the Daimler board of directors to build the newer, faster models, Jellinek agreed to purchase the first 36 examples produced, but with one stipulation, that they be named after his daughter Mercedes. Born in 1889, Mercedes Adrienne Manuela Ramona Jellinek lived a somewhat complicated life, fraught with ill health and two failed marriages to German barons. She died in 1929 at the age of 40. *DaimlerChrysler Classic*

In 1897, after seeing a Daimler advertisement, he paid a visit to the Cannstatt factory. Impressed with what he saw, Jellinek purchased a new two-cylinder Daimler and brought it back to the French Riviera. The motorcar caused quite a stir in Nice and this piqued his salesman's curiosity. He wired Cannstatt and ordered four more cars, with the stipulation that they be so equipped as to reach a top speed of 25 miles per hour, 10 miles per hour faster than the model he had just purchased. Daimler and Maybach complied, although against their better judgment, as such an engine was deemed too powerful for the car's design. Nevertheless, they were built and delivered to Jellinek.

The crafty Austrian merchant already had a plan. Every morning, the Baron Arthur de Rothschild, who spent his winters vacationing on the Riviera, raced his French Panhard motor carriage up to the top of La Turbie hill, and one bright morning Jellinek was there waiting for him behind the tiller of a Daimler.[1] Driving the 15-mile per hour model, he sped past the Baron and scaled the hill. When he caught up with Jellinek, Rothschild was so exasperated by the incident that he purchased the Daimler on the spot. Two weeks later Jellinek overtook Rothschild once again with one of the newer 25-mile per hour Daimlers, which the Baron purchased without delay. Jellinek's little cat and mouse game continued until Rothschild had purchased three of the four cars! At this point Jellinek decided to become a Daimler dealer. He placed an order for an additional six cars, to be equipped with even more powerful four-cylinder engines and built in the style of the latest Phoenix and Daimler-engined Panhards, which had their motors affixed in front, as Jellinek noted in his order, where they should be, as the horse pulls the wagon.

This new request again troubled Daimler and Maybach, as they believed the new four-cylinder engine would be too heavy for the Phoenix, which was powered by a twin in-line engine. Panhard, however, had mounted a Daimler V2 engine in their similarly designed front-engine model with no ill effects, so once again they built what their new "dealer" in Nice requested. These too sold, and in 1899 Jellinek demanded that an even faster 28-horsepower Phoenix be built, which he intended to race during Nice Week in 1900.

By this time Gottlieb Daimler was bed-ridden, and far too ill to be concerned with the day-to-day operation of DMG. Maybach, along with Daimler's son, Paul, made the decision to build an even more powerful

Phoenix model for Jellinek. This time, the result was disaster. On April 30, at the Nice-La Turbie hillclimb, Daimler factory foreman and accomplished race driver Wilhelm Bauer (who had been commissioned by Jellinek to drive the new 28-horsepower model) was unable to maintain control of the unwieldy Phoenix in the first curve and spun the car into a boulder. His mechanic was thrown clear, but the following day Bauer died of his injuries. With Gottlieb Daimler having succumbed to heart failure only weeks before, news of the tragedy in Nice was almost overwhelming. Jellinek laid blame for the accident not on Bauer but on the design of the Phoenix, which he now said was inadequate for the engine power. Maybach must surely have sworn at that!

Despite the loss of Bauer, Jellinek persisted in his demands for faster cars, cars with better engineering and more stylish coachwork than Daimler was producing. Jellinek defined an automobile with a longer wheelbase, lower center of gravity, and a more powerful engine. Ironically, both Maybach and Daimler's son,

This rarely seen photograph shows Wilhelm Werner (behind the wheel) and Baron Henri de Rothschild in the 1901 35-horsepower Mercedes which Werner drove to victory in the Nice Weeks Trials in 1901. *DaimlerChrysler Classic*

The original Cannstatt werke outside Stuttgart in 1900. The popularity of the early front-engine Daimler motorcars was such that production was brisk even before the Mercedes. Pictured are a number of models evolved from the 1897 V-2 Phoenix design. *DaimlerChrysler Classic*

Paul, shared similar beliefs. They had, in fact been working on a design that would cut the weight of the car in half, so that a slight increase in horsepower could result in a significantly faster and better handling automobile. But these were conservative times, and the Daimler board of directors had reservations, especially after Bauer's fatal accident. Unrelenting, Jellinek agreed to purchase the first 36 examples of the new model if DMG would build it, a value of 550,000 Goldmarks (around $130,000 in 1900), an offer even the board of directors couldn't afford to refuse. Then Jellinek added two more stipulations to the financial arrangements. First, he was to be granted the exclusive rights to sell Daimler motorcars in Austria-Hungary, France, Belgium, and America under a profit sharing agreement wth DMG. Secondly, the new motorcars would not be called Daimlers. They were to be named after Jellinek's

The new Untertürkheim factory was very modern compared to the old Cannstatt werke, as was the Mercedes to the earlier front-engine Phoenix. Factory workers posed for this shot in 1906 to depict the attention to detail given every Mercedes motorcar. *DaimlerChrysler Classic*

In Mannheim, the Benz & Co. factory was equally busy turning out new models in the first years of the twentieth century. Pictured is a line of open Tourers on the assembly line. Many of these cars would find their way into American carriage houses through the Benz & Co. importer in New York City. *DaimlerChrysler Classic*

10-year-old daughter, Mercedes, a Spanish Christian name meaning *grace*.

Improbable as this all sounds, Daimler management agreed to the conditions. The 1901 models were equipped with a new more powerful engine; a longer, lower chassis; and stylish, if not trend-setting coachwork. And they were named Mercedes.

The first car was delivered to Jellinek in December 1900 and quickly suffered a series of minor mechanical problems, which were all attended to in time for the 1901 Nice Week in March. Weighing just 2,200 pounds, half that of the previous model, and powered by a 5.9-liter T-head four-cylinder engine producing 35 horsepower, the car was able to ascend La Turbi at an unprecedented speed of 31.9 miles per hour and drive flat out in the distance race at a breathtaking 55 miles per hour! Nothing else even came close. It was revolutionary. Here among these slow, motorized carriages was this magnificent Mercedes with speed. Everyone, even Jellinek, was in awe of the car with its front-mounted engine, low, sleek chassis, and unparalleled performance. Its reputation made by dominating the competitions during Nice Week, the 1901 was hailed as the first modern automobile. It became the foundation on which almost every design since the turn of the century has been based: four road wheels, pressed steel (instead of wood) chassis, honeycomb radiator in front of the engine, gatechange gear lever, driven rear wheels, a front seat for driver and passenger, and rear seat for passengers. It is a simple formula, which has prevailed with few changes for 100 years.

The benchmark one could use to judge the far-reaching influence of the Mercedes on motorcar designs of that period is the Curved-Dash Olds, also introduced in 1901. Proclaimed by builder Ransom Eli Olds as America's first production motor carriage, the Curved-Dash was small, simple in its execution, and very similar to late nineteenth century European models like the Benz Velo. And like the Benz, it, too, was all but obsolete in comparison to the Mercedes. Fortunately for Olds, few Americans could make that comparison, and the Curved-Dash Olds became the best-selling motorcar in America during the early 1900s. However, half a world away, Wilhelm Maybach and Emil Jellinek had changed the course of automotive history with the Mercedes. Perhaps unaware of the overwhelming significance of his statement or the role that the automobile would

This original wheel lug has taken its knocks over the last century, but still clearly denotes the Daimler name and Cannstatt werke.

play in the development of twentieth century civilization, French motor journalist Paul Meyan wrote in his review of the events at Nice, *Nous sommes entres dans l'ere Mercedes.* "We have entered the Mercedes era." In 1902 so did DMG, officially registering the name as a trademark. In 1903, Jellinek was so bold as to have his family name legally changed to Jellinek-Mercedes!

Maybach made further improvements to the 1901 design, which became the Mercedes Simplex the following year. The newer model had an even lower, longer stance, and a 40-horsepower engine capable of speeds exceeding a mile a minute. When the Mercedes Simplex made its debut at the Paris Salon, the motoring world was stunned a second time in as many years. *The Automobile* magazine of Great Britain noted, "Mr. Maybach, of Cannstatt, across the Rhine, has led the way to a new epoch in automobile construction and has compelled the world to follow."[2]

With the success of the Mercedes, production demands began to outstrip the capabilities of Daimler's

Fuel pressurizing hand pump was mounted to the firewall alongside a pressure gauge. It was generally the front seat passenger's job to keep the pressure up and the fuel flowing to the carburetor.

FAR LEFT:
Until about 1910 a number of different models were constructed at DMG on the basis of the Simplex design. Some were given the name Simplex, such as this 1907, while others were designated as 35-horsepower models from 1905 to 1909 when the name was changed to 22/35-horsepower. A windshield was not a standard feature in 1907!

Cannstatt headquarters, and the company moved to a larger facility in the Untertürkheim district of Stuttgart. Production at the old Cannstatt Werk continued until the building was razed by fire on June 10, 1903, and everything, including 90 vehicles, was lost, among them three 90-horsepower race cars for the Gordon Bennett race.

The 1900s marked the beginning of an era when enterprise and progress in the development of personal transportation advanced by leaps and bounds, from mere single-cylinder motor-driven carriages, barely able to keep pace with a horse and buggy, to automobiles capable of speeds of more than 60 miles per hour. Traveling at a mile a minute was once believed impossible without risk to life and limb, and until the advent of

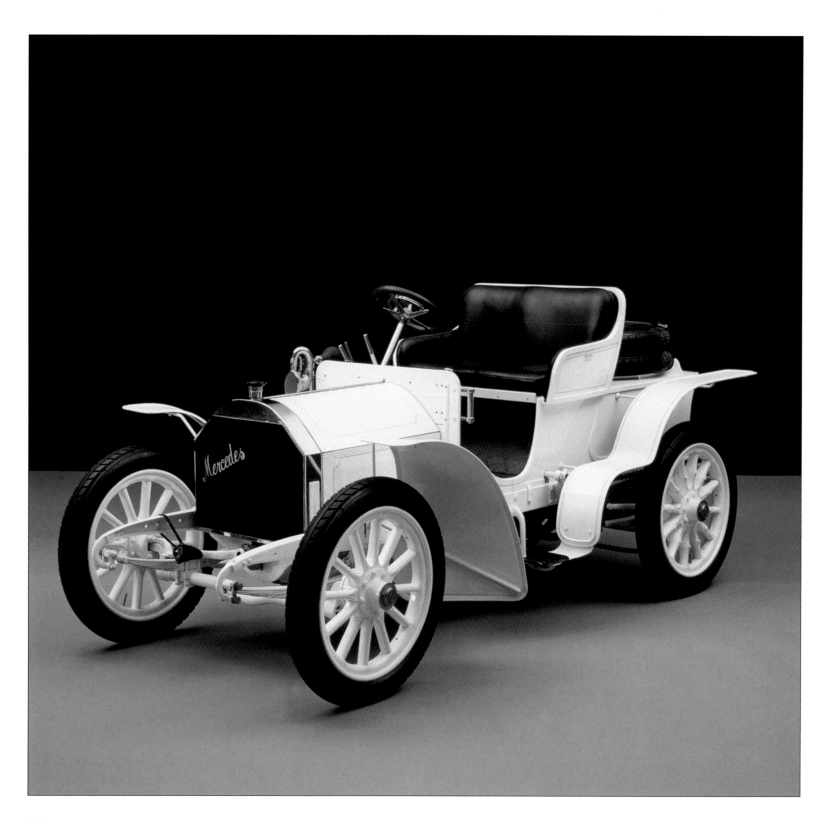

the Mercedes, that wasn't far from the truth. By 1903, just two years after the first 35-horsepower model had been introduced at Nice Week, Daimler was offering a 60-horsepower Mercedes, and later that year would introduce the Mercedes 90. The name, as it implies, was representative of the automobile's horsepower rating, nearly three times that of the 1901 model. Daimler's customers were no longer satisfied with a motorcar that could reach 60 miles per hour. The cry was for 70 miles per hour, then 85, and the voice of a few arose whose fervent desire was to race down the wind at 100 miles per hour. Mercedes would not disappoint them.

The meteoric success of the Mercedes in the early years of the twentieth century spelled disaster for Benz, whose entire model line had been rendered obsolete virtually overnight. Sales plummeted in 1901 and again in 1902, yet Karl Benz still refused to change the design of his vehicles, believing his little belt-driven cars would prevail. They would not. By 1903 change was at last on the horizon at Benz & Co. with the introduction of the new Parsifal model, a design remarkably similar in most respects to the latest Mercedes. Thus began a rivalry between the cars from Mannheim and those from Stuttgart, a battle between men and machines that would be waged on both road and track for more than 20 years, turning the 1910s and early 1920s into one of the most exciting periods in European motoring history.

Paul Meyan had been wrong. We had entered the Mercedes and Benz era.

CHAPTER THREE

Early Benz and Mercedes Models

The Motorcar Comes of Age

Having built the most advanced motorcar of the new century, what Daimler needed next was a suitable trademark to complement it. Paul and Adolf Daimler, who were now managers at their father's company, recalled that he had once sent a picture to their mother on which a star marked the house where they lived outside Cologne, during his years as technical director at Gasmotorenfabrik Deutz. He had commented that eventually this star "will shine down on us and our children and, I hope, bring us good fortune." DMG's new chairman, Alfred von Kaulla, took the idea up and in June 1909 applied to use both a three-pointed star and a four-pointed star as trademarks. Both applications were granted, but only the three-pointed star was used, originally placed at the front of the car as a radiator emblem. Over the years the star acquired various

The 37/95 could also be bodied in a slightly more formal fashion, such as this variation of the Sports Touring body fitted with dual windscreen, sidemount spares, and spotlight.

additions and refinements. It was placed inside a circle in 1916, creating the first Mercedes badge, and in 1921 it evolved into the three-pointed star within the ring, which in countless variations over the decades has become the marque's eternal symbol, along with the laurel wreath border adapted from the original Benz emblem in 1926.

As the world raced headlong into the twentieth century, there was growth in virtually every area of industry, and DMG and Benz were now heatedly competing for sales, not only in Europe, but the United States, which was becoming a lucrative market for imported motorcars. At Daimler, the acrimony that had been growing between Paul Daimler and Wilhelm Maybach had finally become too much for the 60-year-old engineer to endure. Following a lengthy disagreement with Paul over the design of the 1906 Daimler race car, he decided to retire. In April 1907 Maybach left the company he had helped bring into being in 1890.

The problems that had arisen between Paul Daimler and Maybach were perhaps more politically motivated than personal. The Daimler brothers, Paul and Adolf, now sought to gain top management positions within the company. Paul had returned to Stuttgart after a tenure as chief engineer at Austro-Daimler, and with Maybach's departure was appointed chief engineer of Daimler-Motoren-Gesellschaft. Younger brother Adolf, who had always been close to Maybach, stepped into the position of factory manager.

Over at Austro-Daimler, a young German engineer named Ferdinand Porsche was promoted to the position vacated by Paul Daimler, thus setting into motion events that would lead to Porsche's rise within DMG by the early 1920s.

As for Wilhelm Maybach, afternoon tea and retirement were not what he had in mind when he departed from Daimler. Having pioneered the development of the first motor-powered dirigible in 1888, Maybach joined forces with Graf Ferdinand von Zeppelin in the development of a new aero engine for Zeppelin's giant airships, which had been powered by Daimler engines since 1900. Maybach was given responsibility for overseeing the construction of all-new engines and his son, Karl (a gifted engineer in his own right), was appointed technical director. A separate company, Luftfahrzeug-Motorenbau GmbH (changed in 1912 to Maybach Motorenbau Gesellschaft), was established to produce the Zeppelin engines, and it would be from the

M.M.G. factory in Friedrichshafen, Germany, that the first Maybach automobiles would emerge following World War I.

About the same time Maybach was shown the door, Herr Jellinek-Mercedes also found himself on an outbound road, having fallen in great disfavor with DMG management over his boasts of being the Mercedes designer. In a letter to the esteemed German motoring publication *Allgemeine Automobil-Zeitung,* Jellinek wrote ". . . not only the whole business, but also the whole construction of the Mercedes car, was and still is entirely built on my plans." That was in 1906. A year later he was emphatically on the outs with the Daimler organization and decided it was time to *retire* from the business. His name and integrity, though, were well intact, at least for the moment. Archduke Franz Ferdinand, heir to the Austrian throne (and whose assassination in Sarajevo on June 28, 1914, would trigger World War I), had Jellinek-Mercedes appointed honorary vice consul in

Monaco, a title and position suitable to his pompous nature. Unfortunately, Jellinek's new quasi-political status landed him on the wrong side when the battle lines were drawn. Accused of espionage by the French, he fled to Switzerland, where he would remain in exile. In his absence, the Villa Mercedes, Jellinek's personal properties, yachts, and automobiles were all confiscated. Everything was gone. In January 1918, Emil Jellinek died in Switzerland, never to know the outcome of the war to end all wars, or the future of the motorcars that bore his daughter's name.

As the first decade of the new century neared its end, Ransom E. Olds and Henry Ford were building automobiles for the masses—Henry's Model T put America on wheels and would drive the price of most

Barney Oldfield, who had come out of retirement to attempt a land speed record with the Blitzen Benz at Daytona in 1910, barnstormed with the car throughout the year, spreading the Benz name from coast to coast. *DaimlerChrysler Classic*

The Blitzen Benz pictured as it appeared in 1911 after being reworked for its attempt at the land speed record. The Blitzen Benz was as close to a projectile as any automobile could have come. The least aerodynamic aspect of the car was the driver and mechanic! *DaimlerChrysler Classic*

Mercedes' most significant racing victory of the pre–World War I era was the 1914 French Grand Prix at Le Mans, in which the team finished 1-2-3, with Christian Lautenschlager first in car Number 28, Otto Salzer second in car Number 39, and Louis Wagner third in car Number 40. *DaimlerChrysler Classic*

models below $1,000 by 1910. The Mercedes and the Benz, on the other hand, were among the most expensive motorcars one could buy in America. Benz chassis prices ranged from $3,250 for the 18-horsepower model up to $8,500 for the sporty 60-horsepower versions. In comparison, a new Model T sold for $900, and that was a complete car, not a bare chassis still in need of coachwork!

Through the Benz Auto Import Co. of America, in New York City, the entire Benz model line was offered with a selection of four different chassis and 16 coach-built bodies. They were in the opinion of many the best motorcars of the era, from either side of the Atlantic. Better than the Cadillac, Pierce-Arrow, or Packard. Better than a Rolls-Royce. Better even than the Mercedes.

Benz & Co. had earned its stripes with American buyers in 1910 with a double victory in the U.S. Grand Prix at Savannah, Georgia, with drivers David L. Bruce Brown and Victor Héméry finishing 1-2 in their 150-horsepower Benz race cars. In 1910, Benz also set the world land speed record, with none other than American racing legend Barney Oldfield streaking across the hard-packed Ormond-Daytona Beach sand behind the wheel of a 200-horsepower Lightning Benz (later

known as the Blitzen Benz). Said Oldfield, who was never short of self- aggrandizing quotes, of his record run, "A speed of 131 miles an hour is as near to the absolute limit of speed as humanity will ever travel." At the time it was very close to the truth. Wrote the *Florida Times Union* of Oldfield's official 131.724-mile per hour record run, "The speed attained was the fastest ever traveled by a human being, no greater speed having been recorded except that made by a bullet."[1] It was a record that would stand for only one year. In 1911 race driver Bob Burman piloted the Blitzen Benz to a top speed of 141.732 miles per hour at Daytona, a full 10 miles per hour faster than Oldfield.

When the news reached Germany, no doubt the beer steins were raised in Mannheim by everyone at Benz & Co., with the possible exception of Karl Benz, who was perhaps the least enthusiastic of anyone when it came to building sports and racing cars. The passion in Mannheim was being fueled by his sons Richard and Eugen, by company engineer and driver Victor Héméry, and chief engineer Hans Nibel, who quietly overlooked the old man's view of racing cars, or for that matter, any car with a top speed above 50 kilometers per hour, as "nonsense."

The 200-horsepower Blitzen Benz was the latest version of the 1908 Benz Grand Prix cars that had

The variety of models offered by Mercedes in the 1910s ran the gamut from mild-mannered Tourenwagens like this 1910 22/40 model . . .

come in second and third in the Grand Prix de France, at Le Mans, crossing the finish line just moments behind a new Mercedes. Benz & Co. was like a sleeping giant that had been rudely awakened, and now sought to vanquish its antagonist. By 1910, Benz had its own branches in France, Belgium, Great Britain, Italy, Austria, and Hungary, and was the majority stockholder in the Benz Auto Import Co. of America. Now it was DMG that had to continually look over its shoulder. In motorsports, wherever Mercedes appeared, there too was Benz, claiming its share of victories on both sides of the Atlantic and setting speed and endurance records.

In 1913, DMG campaigned a Mercedes-Knight, driven by the Belgian Théodor Pilette, in the Indianapolis 500 Mile Sweepstakes Race on May 29. The car finished a respectable fifth. In 1915, American Ralph de Palma would win the Indy 500 driving a 1914 Mercedes Grand Prix car, which oddly enough belonged to Packard. De Palma's winning Indy pit crew had been headed by none other than Packard's chief engineer Col. Jesse Vincent!

Paul Daimler designed a series of competition models that were raced at Le Mans in August 1913 (not in the Grand Prix event, however) finishing third (with Pilette at the wheel), fourth, sixth, and seventh. He then designed five new cars for the 1914 Grand Prix at Le Mans (the last race before the war) where the Mercedes team scored

. . . to exotic-looking Sports Tourers like this 1913 Model 37/95.

The dashboard had yet to be invented and even the finest motorcars carried their gauges on the firewall panel.

Although Mercedes offered a variety of models, chassis, and engines, styling was less varied. This 1916 Tourer was only slightly more advanced in design than models built in 1910. Perhaps the greatest difference was that now all cars were shaft-drive, which served to clean up the body lines by eliminating the exterior chain housings forward of the rear fender. Tires and wheels were also smaller and ground clearance had been reduced.

UPPER RIGHT:
One of the most exotic bodies ever built for the Mercedes 37/90 chassis was this all-mahogany skiff manufactured in 1911 by Jean Henri Labourdette for American hat maker Henry G. Stetson. The car, which cost a staggering $18,000 in 1911, was delivered to Stetson's residence in Elkins Park, outside Philadelphia.

an unprecedented 1-2-3 finish, with Christian Lautenschlager driving the winning car, in what was for its time the most exciting automobile race ever seen in Europe.

The real race between Daimler and Benz, however, was for sales dominance, and in that competition Mercedes and Benz were nearly in a dead heat. In 1910 they both delivered more than 1,000 motorcars, a number that would double for Daimler within two years and triple for Benz. Their respective commercial vehicle operations were also at capacity. Benz and Daimler trucks, buses, and fire engines (as well as aircraft and marine engines) were in use the world over by the beginning of World War I.

There were so many different models offered in the years before the war that Mercedes seemed to be building a different series of cars almost every year. In 1913 Daimler offered a total of 12 different chassis, 4 with conventional chain-driven rear axles and 8 with shaft drive. Of those, 3 models were fitted with the new sleeve valve-design engine licensed in 1910 from American engineer Charles Knight. Still, the most powerful car in the Mercedes lineup was the 37/95-horsepower, utilizing the proven poppet valve four-cylinder engine and conventional chain-drive.

The most spectacular of all Mercedes motorcars prior to World War I, were the 37/90-horsepower introduced in 1911 and 37/95-horsepower of 1913, offered in three different wheelbase lengths, 3,380 millimeters (133 inches), 3,525 millimeters (139 inches), and 3,580

millimeters (141 inches) with a 1,450-millimeter (57-inch) track. Average dimensions were 4,870–5,100 millimeters by 1,750 millimeters by 1,600 millimeters—from 192 inches to 200 inches in length, 69 inches in width, and 63 inches in overall height, respectively. Later models produced from 1912 to 1914 had a slightly wider track of 1,520 millimeters (60 inches). The 37/95-horsepower was followed briefly in 1915 by an even more powerful 38/100-horsepower model. The actual horsepower of the engines, incidentally, was always the second number listed, the first, based on the displacement figure was used solely for taxation purposes.

At this point in DMG history, Mercedes offered their motorcars with a choice of either the new shaft-drive system, designed by Paul Daimler in 1907 and 1908, or the original chain-drive variant, and while the latter was being phased out, in 1911 the factory introduced a new chain-driven car, including the 37/90-horsepower model. While less sophisticated, and considerably noisier, chain-drive had proven more reliable than shaft-driven cars when they were equipped with larger, more powerful engines, such as the 37/90-horsepower.

As the most expensive model available, production was never significant, and in 1913 only 1,567 chassis of all types were produced, accounting for the 10/25, 14/35, 22/50, 28/60, 38/80, 37/90-horsepower poppet valve models, as well as the 10/30, 16/45 and 25/65 Knight models.

In the 1910s, Mercedes styling ran the gamut from conservative Limousines and Landaulets to dashing Phaetons and high-spirited sport two-seaters. Daring designs such as the black Sport-Phaeton shown in this chapter were among the most popular, offering either a formal or sporty guise depending on whether the large fabric top was folded. This was perhaps the most flamboyant factory model for 1913, save for the two-seat Sport-Zweisitzer, and since the 37/95 engines were also considered suitable for racing, a handful of chassis were

bodied with lightweight, Rennsport-Zweisitzer (racing two-seater) coachwork as well.

The 37/90 and 37/95 models were distinguished, as were many models, by their massive vee-radiator shells (which would become a Mercedes-Benz trademark in the late 1920s and throughout the 1930s), and on the most expensive models, stunning nickel silver headlamps mirroring the car's majestic prow. (A similar car can be seen on page 107 of Werner Oswald's *Mercedes-Benz-Personenwagen* listed as a 1913 Mercedes 37/90 Sport-Phaeton.)

Although not unique to the 37/90 and 37/95 series, the bold, exposed, polished exhaust pipes pouring through the left side of the hood and curving along the body added to the dazzling appearance of the big Mercedes. In addition, the dashing lines of the Sport-Phaeton body style were often emphasized further by the conspicuous absence of a windshield, although at this point a windshield was regarded as standard equipment on all but competition cars.

Throughout the period leading up to and after World War I, both Benz and Mercedes models grew in popularity with literally hundreds of different designs being created between them. It was truly an era of sweeping changes and technological achievements, as the motorcar evolved from a turn-of-the-century curiosity into one of the most celebrated inventions of modern time.

The magnificent 90-horsepower Mercedes four-cylinder engine displaced 9.5 liters (nearly 600 ci) and was composed of two blocks of two cylinders with the valvetrains in each controlled by a single cam located in the crankcase.

The link between road car and race car came for Benz in 1908 with the Grand Prix design powered by a four-cylinder engine producing 158 horsepower!

CHAPTER FOUR

The 1920s—Daimler and Benz Become One

Ferdinand Porsche Leads a Renaissance

The sound of a supercharged Mercedes-Benz
engine was once compared to a concert performed
by the Trumpets of Jericho.

War is a political battle fought by everyone but politicians. World War I was to bring about tremendous change within the automotive industry, both in America and in Europe, where the potential of the motorcar was realized for the first time in history as more than a means of personal transportation. Beverly Rae Kimes noted quite poignantly in *The Star and the Laurel* that the awakening came in September 1914, when General Gallieni ordered the use of French taxis to carry troops to the Marne front. The troop transport was born. Armored

The 460 Nürburg chassis was offered with a wide variety of coachwork, from sporty two-seaters to luxurious limousines like this 1929 example bodied by Karosserie Papler in Cologne. The 460 Nürburg chassis (W 08 and 460 K) were manufactured through 1933, with a total production of 2,893. The pressed-steel drop frame platform was offered in two wheelbase lengths: the standard 3,670-millimeter (145-inch) model pictured and a short 3,430-millimeter (135-inch) Kurz sport version.

cars, particularly those produced by Rolls-Royce, played a significant role in battle, and the advent of the tank, perhaps the ultimate armored car, gave the British a marked advantage over the Germans, who found themselves sorely behind in the manufacture of military vehicles. More than a decade before the war, Paul Daimler had tried to interest both the German and Austrian governments in armored military trucks, but neither showed any interest. Now it was DMG that was racing to produce military vehicles for the war effort, staff cars, and aircraft engines by the score, while the Benz plants were turned over largely to submarine and aviation engine work. It was all for naught. When the war ended on November 11, 1918, Germany had not only lost the confrontation but its economy as well.

Race driver and engineer Max Sailer led the Mercedes racing effort in the years prior to Alfred Neubauer coming to Daimler-Benz from Austro-Daimler. Pictured in 1914, Sailer would lead the winning Mercedes team in the 1922 Targa Florio. *DaimlerChrysler Classic*

A rare photo of Alfred Neubauer when he was a much lighter weight than history remembers him, and behind the wheel of a Mercedes race car in the 1924 Targa Florio! To the right is an equally young Ferdinand Porsche. Both men worked together at Austro-Daimler before joining Daimler-Benz. *DaimlerChrysler Classic*

Following the Treaty of Versailles in 1919, the value of the German mark began to plummet. In 1914, before the war, the mark had traded against the U.S. dollar at 4.20 to 1. Now it took 62 marks to equal one U.S. dollar! By 1920 the German automotive industry was on its last legs. Fuel shortages, and the general instability of the economy, saw more cars parked along the side of the road than on it. People were out of work, and both Benz and Daimler were banned by the conditions of the Versailles treaty from any military production, including the manufacture of aircraft engines. The newest DMG plant located in Sindelfingen was being used to build furniture, and automobile production, what there was of it at Daimler, was well under 1,000 units for the first year after the war. The situation was much the same at Benz, which had faired slightly better than Daimler, but was still under 1,000 cars in 1919, an estimated 988 from the Mannheim Werk, plus an additional 800 trucks from the Gaggenau factory.

In addition to Benz and Daimler, there was Horch, Opel, Auto Union, Wanderer, and Adler, among major German automakers all struggling for a share of an almost nonexistent market. In total there were 86 German auto companies offering 144 different models—yet only one German in 280 could even afford to own an automobile! Compounding the difficulties at home was DMG's loss of foreign sales and dealerships in the countries that Germany had fought against. Sentiment was not in their favor, nor in Benz's.

Porsche, at far right, looks on as drivers prepare for their assault on the Targa Florio in 1924. *DaimlerChrysler Classic*

Often in the face of adversity our greatest strengths emerge, and so it was for both Daimler and Benz in the early post–World War I years. At DMG the emphasis was to be on performance and the development of supercharging, while at Benz, engineers were working on the further development of the diesel engine.

In 1921 both Daimler and Benz had new products to display at the first postwar Berlin Automobile Show. Beneath the Silver Star banner were two new supercharged sports models, each with a four-cylinder single-overhead cam engine. The first car in the world to be offered with a supercharger as standard equipment, the new Mercedes received immediate acceptance on both sides of the Atlantic, and as old wounds healed over the battles fought between Germany, France, England, and America, the foreign market once again began to open

The amalgamation of Benz and Daimler immediately produced a number of exceptional motorcars, such as this 1926 Model 630 "K" engineered by Ferdinand Porsche. Coachwork on this stylish example was created in France by Jacques Saoutchik. *DaimlerChrysler Classic*

its doors. Benz and Daimler were making money, but not enough.

Restrictions on Germany were still severe, travel outside the country was difficult, and inflation was running rampant in the early 1920s. A new Benz had to sell for 25 million marks! Not that it amounted to much. A mark was worth about one penny against the U.S. dollar and by 1923, as Ferry Porsche (the son of Prof. Ferdinand Porsche) noted in his book *Cars Are My Life*, ". . . one U.S. dollar was worth 354.00 marks." Germany's economy was crumbling. By October 1923 the German mark was almost worthless. Recalled Porsche: "One day I was given 10 million marks for my tram fare to school. That was enough to get me into town but I did not have enough money for the return journey and had to walk home."

For the 1926 model year, Ferdinand Porsche had revamped the earlier 630, designed by Paul Daimler, giving the car better handling through chassis revisions and greater performance with an improved six-cylinder supercharged engine. A view without coachwork is one seldom seen by anyone but a restorer. *DaimlerChrysler Classic*

The chassis line at Daimler-Benz in Untertürkheim shortly after the merger. Shown are the new Model K units on their individual rolling carriers. *DaimlerChrysler Classic*

Germany's financial problems were assuaged by a new national currency introduced in November 1923, immediately becoming legal tender at an exchange rate of 4.2 billion paper marks for one rentenmark. This provided the foundation upon which the German economy slowly began to recover. However, it was not as easy to find a solution to the country's ailing automotive industry.

In the French Grand Prix at Le Mans, the most important race in Europe and perhaps in the world, German cars were not welcome. Thus racing, the great public venue that had helped establish the prewar reputations of both Daimler and Benz, was denied them, for surely had the German cars appeared at the *Circuit de La Sarthe*, they would have been triumphant.

In 1923, Ferdinand Porsche had arrived from Austro-Daimler to assume the position of chief engineer at DMG, following Paul Daimler's decision to leave the company and pursue a position as chief engineer with Horch—one of the four rings that would form the great German Auto Union in 1932. The first of the great sports car created by Ferdinand Porsche was the Targa

Florio race car in 1924 followed by two six-cylinder supercharged touring cars, the 15/70/100-horsepower and the 24/100/140-horsepower, in December 1924.

Having already agreed in principle to a mutually beneficial sharing of resources in the early postwar years, by 1924 the two struggling automakers found

Stabilimenti Farina (a forerunner of Pininfarina, which was established by Battista "Pinin" Farina, the youngest of the Farina brothers) also bodied early Mercedes-Benz chassis, like this 1926 model fitted with formal coachwork.
DaimlerChrysler Classic

The Mercedes-Benz Type S was the first completely new model from the newly merged concern. With a 6.8-liter supercharged six-cylinder engine and an improved chassis design engineered by Ferdinand Porsche, the S became one of the most powerful and desirable automobiles on both sides of the Atlantic. American song and dance man Al Jolson was an early S owner, shown here with his 1927 Sport model Tourer.
DaimlerChrysler Classic

Foreign coachbuilders rendered some exceptional designs for the Model S and SS, such as this striking SS Cabriolet bodied in Italy by Carrozzeria Castagna in 1928. *DaimlerChrysler Classic*

The Model S and SS chassis was the finest sports car platform of its time. Pictured is a factory display SS chassis. The exceptional workmanship was no less on the regular production cars, including the hand-crafted, engine-turned finishes on the cylinder head, manifold, supercharger, and engine compartment panels. *DaimlerChrysler Classic*

themselves being forced closer and closer together by necessity, and on May 1 they entered into an *Agreement of Mutual Interest*, a noncompetitive and cooperative arrangement, which served as a prelude to their merger two years later, in June 1926. The formation of Daimler-Benz AG consolidated their engineering and production capabilities into the largest automobile manufacturing company in Germany. Although initially the two firms retained their individual identity, as time wore on there came the need for Benz & Co. and Daimler-Motoren-Gesellschaft to become one and the same.

The first product of Daimler-Benz AG, aside from the little changed, traditional, lower-priced Mannheim and Stuttgart models, was the Model K, introduced in 1926. The Model K was more an evolutionary design than a completely new luxury automobile. Based upon the Type 630 Mercedes 24/100/140 PS introduced in 1924, it was principally the work of Porsche and his predecessor Paul Daimler. Porsche improved upon Daimler's pioneering overhead camshaft six-cylinder engine design and Roots-type supercharger, giving the massive K models unparalleled straight-line performance. Specified by

Daimler-Benz to attain a top speed of 90 miles per hour, it was the fastest standard production model of its type in the world.

The supercharger was the foundation for an entirely new and more powerful generation of Mercedes that would emerge in the late 1920s and flourish throughout the 1930s. The Roots supercharger, however, was not invented for the automobile! In fact, it is older. When brothers Francis and Philander Roots patented a blower in 1860, they had no idea their invention would play an integral role in the development of the motorcar. At the time, the only thing the two Connersville, Indiana, inventors had in mind was improving the performance of the water turbine for their spinning mill. The design, however, laid the groundwork for the Roots-type superchargers used to this day throughout the automotive industry. Paul Daimler built the first example shortly after World War I. Having gained some experience with supercharging aircraft engines, he attempted to fit a Roots-type blower to the Knight sleeve-valve engine of a Mercedes 16/50 horsepower model, which proved to be an unsuitable host. Continued experiments with the larger 7.3-liter six used in the 28/95 series were successful, and in 1922 Max Sailer drove the first supercharged Mercedes race car to victory in the Targa Florio.

Daimler's 28/95 Sport "Targa Florio" was powered by a modified aircraft engine. Introduced in 1914 the model was inspired by the aero-engined sixes that had raced at Le Mans in 1913. Except for modifications necessary for automotive installation, the six used in the 28/95 series was identical to the Daimler DF80 aircraft engine. The production of the 28/95 resumed after World War I, and in 1922, Max Sailer drove one to a second place finish in the Targa Florio, behind Count Giulio Masetti, also driving a Mercedes.

The theoretical operation of the Roots blower is similar to that of a gear pump. Instead of using gears that mesh, however, two counterrotating cylindrical rollers with figure-eight-shaped cross sections feed the gas. The cylinders operate with a minimum aperture in a housing, the inside of which comprises two connected semicircles. As the cylinders spin, the gases are compressed, due to the feed pressure. The supercharger itself is driven by the engine's crankshaft, and in a model like the 630 K, for example, was geared to rotate at a greater speed than the engine. Installed ahead of the carburetor, it forced precompressed air into the carburetor, which was then enriched with the fuel. The net result was more horsepower, although the supercharger could only be engaged for short periods of time without

causing damage to the engine. But in that brief span when the engine wailed, a supercharged Mercedes was breathtaking both in sight and sound. As Mercedes-Benz so poignantly noted in *The Fascination of the Compressor*, a 1998 book on the history of the company's supercharged cars, "[in the 1920s and 1930s] the sound and appearance of the Mercedes-Benz engines were testimony to the raw power beneath the hood. This was innovative technology encased in the most elegant car bodies of the time. The high-gloss chrome exhaust pipes that peeked from the side of the hood became synonymous with superchargers, the symbol of power and glory. These mighty machines were like creatures from ancient legends. The only way to escape their beguiling melody, their aura, their fascination, was to hide yourself away

The Model SS was triumphant at the Nürburgring in 1928 with a stunning 1-2-3 finish by Caracciola, Otto Merz (pictured) and Christian Werner.
DaimlerChrysler Classic

The SS model was the successor to the S. During the six years that the SS was manufactured, the output of the 7.1-liter engine increased from 200 horsepower up to 225 horsepower with the supercharger engaged.
DaimlerChrysler Classic

The final evolution of the S series was the lightweight SSKL. Notable changes were the drilled out frame and significantly increased performance from the inline six-cylinder engine, which in the SSKL developed 240 horsepower normally aspirated and a staggering 300 horsepower with the supercharger at full cry.
DaimlerChrysler Classic

Early advertisements presenting the merger of Daimler and Benz as Mercedes-Benz.

NEXT PAGE:
The Model K was more an evolutionary design than a completely new luxury automobile. Based upon the Type 630 Mercedes 24/100/140 PS introduced in 1924, it was principally the work of chief engineer Dr. Ferdinand Porsche who improved upon Paul Daimler's overhead camshaft six-cylinder engine design and Roots-type supercharger, giving the massive K models unparalleled straight-line performance. Specified by DBAG to attain 90 miles per hour, it was the fastest standard model of its type in the world.

and stop up your ears." Such was the image Mercedes-Benz had fashioned for itself.

As to the road manners of the new Model K, any change from the earlier 630, however small, would have to be considered an improvement. The stiff underpinnings—semielliptic leaf springs at all four corners and cumbersome channel-section chassis—of the older model had imparted all the characteristics of a truck. The K introduced an improved suspension design on a shorter wheelbase, 134 inches compared with the 630's 147.5-inch span. The "K" designation in this specific instance stood for Kurz (German for short), rather than for Kompressor (supercharged) as on later Mercedes-Benz models utilizing the "K" classification, such as the 540 K.

With less overall weight on a more responsive suspension, Dr. Porsche could also increase the output of Daimler's supercharged six, which had previously made 100 horsepower with an additional 40 horsepower delivered when the supercharger was engaged by depressing the throttle pedal fully to the floor. The improved six made 110/160 horsepower. The supercharged models

also marked a departure from the earlier method of differentiating taxable horsepower and brake horsepower. With the new models, dual figures denoted standard output and supercharged. (When three figures were shown, the first was now for tax purposes.)

The increased power came from a higher compression ratio (5.0:1, up from 4.7:1) and better ignition through Ferdinand Porsche's use of two spark plugs per cylinder. With a bore and stroke of 94x150 millimeters (3-11/16x5-29/32 inches), the K's engine displaced 6.24 liters (381 ci). One of the few carryovers from the old 630 was the four-speed gearbox with straight-cut gears and a 1:1 ratio in top. As a transitional model during the Daimler and Benz consolidation, the K proved to be an excellent luxury alternative to the sporting S, SS, and SSK series that Porsche would create in the 1920s. The S series was particularly successful in racing, and with drivers such as Rudolf Caracciola, Christian Werner, Otto Merz, Manfred von Brauchitsch, Adolf Rosenberger, and Hans Stuck, achieved many important international successes for Daimler-Benz.

The right-hand-drive chassis beneath this car was one of the first produced in the new 1928 Nürburg series. Unlike the Stuttgart and Mannheim models, named for the factories where they were produced, or the supercharged "S" Sport, "SS" Super Sport, "SSK" Super Sport Kurz, and "SSKL" Super-Sport-Kurz-Leicht models, named for their chassis, the Nürburg 460 was named after the Nürburgring racing circuit. Mercedes tested the new 460 straight-eight by putting a preproduction prototype through a punishing 13-day, nonstop endurance run, covering a distance of 12,500 miles, while maintaining an average speed of 40.5 miles per hour. The record-setting 311-hour trial virtually doubled the time and distance previously achieved by a factory stock car, after which Mercedes christened the car the 460 Nürburg.

FAR RIGHT:
The Model S was built on a new drop-center frame with a 133-inch wheelbase. To improve the handling over the Model K, Porsche had the radiator and engine repositioned about a foot rearward on the chassis, resulting in better front/rear weight distribution and a lower center of gravity. This lower chassis also encouraged more rakish open coachwork on the Model S, such as the Touring body pictured, designed by Gangloff and built by Zeitz in 1927 for American entertainer Al Jolson.

The Model S and subsequent SS and SSK were built on a new drop-center frame with a 133-inch standard wheelbase. To improve the handling over the Model K, the new design moved the radiator and engine about a foot rearward on the chassis, resulting in better front/rear weight distribution and a lower center of gravity. This lower chassis also encouraged more rakish, open coachwork.

With chassis improvements came greater performance, 120 horsepower under normal aspiration, 180 with the supercharger engaged. The updated engine in the Model S, the single strongest tie to Daimler, had its bore increased from 94 to 98 millimeters. With a 150-millimeter stroke, this brought displacement up to 6,789 cc, about 414 ci. The SSK, powered by a 170/225-horsepower (increased to 180/250 horsepower in 1929) Roots supercharged inline six, was capable of reaching the magic century mark. Every builder of luxury cars at the time claimed to achieve this speed; Mercedes actually did. Racing versions with higher-compression engines running on Elcosine—an alcohol/fuel mixture used for competition—attained speeds well in excess of 100 miles per hour. In one of these competition versions, Rudolf Caracciola surpassed 120 miles per hour in the 1927 Belgian Speed Trial, and won the opening event of the Nurbürgring. The culmination of the S Series was the

Competition models of the SS, like this 1930 Type 710 SS, helped Rudolf Caracciola earn the title of European Sports Car Champion in 1930 and European Mountain Champion in 1930 and 1931. The competition coachwork for this example was produced in England by the firm of Forrest-Lycett.

SSKL, which appeared in 1931, a lighter and more powerful version purpose built for motor sports, but equally at home on the open road.

Production of the supercharged S or Sport (180-horsepower) model was limited to 128 chassis; another 111 SS or Super Sport (with the improved 7.1-liter 200- to 225-horsepower engine) models were built; a scant 33 SSK (250-horsepower, short-wheelbase) examples were built; and just 7 SSKL (300-horsepower) competition versions were produced, none of which have survived. This was the factory tally for the entire Model S series produced from 1927 to 1934.

Off the track, nearly all Model S body styles were of the open touring design, but very traditional, severe, and upright in appearance. The majority of bodies were

This Mercedes Boattail Speedster was commissioned in 1928 by Howard Isham of Santa Barbara, California, with the coachwork designed and built by the Walter M. Murphy Company in Pasadena. As far as can be determined, only one Boattail Speedster was ever built on an SSK chassis, and of the entire SSK production, roughly 31 cars, only two were bodied outside of Europe and Great Britain; the second, also by Murphy, was a Cabriolet built for Zeppo Marx.

The SSK was the most popular sports model produced in the late 1920s (the SSKL primarily being deemed a race car), although with examples such as this 1927 Roadster, the line separating SSK and SSKL was a thin one indeed.

55

The most famous SSK ever built is this stunning sports racer originally owned by Count Carlo Felice Trossi. An Italian aristocrat whose family lineage dated back to the fourteenth century, Trossi was a proficient race driver and president of Scuderia Ferrari in the early 1930s. The SSK, Chassis Number 36038, was built in 1930 but not purchased until 1932. Although the body lacks a builder's plate, it is believed that the coachwork for the Trossi SSK was by Jacques Saoutchik— while the Trossi family says that the work was done by a little-known English panel beater named Willy White, who was living in Italy, and that the body was designed by Trossi himself. Following Trossi's untimely death in 1949, the car changed hands numerous times, finally becoming part of the Tom Perkins collection, which was later purchased by internationally renowned designer and clothier Ralph Lauren. The Trossi SSK has won at every major Concours d'Elegance at which it has appeared, including Pebble Beach in 1993, and is considered one of the most beautiful cars in the world.

designed and manufactured by the Sindelfingen Werk, but S Series chassis were also fitted with coachwork designed by the leading German Karosseriewerk —Erdmann & Rossi, Papler, and in Geneva, Switzerland, at Zeitz.

Apart from the normal touring bodies were several sport-touring types with cut-down doors and more rakish lines. The Sindelfingen Werk built a stylish *tourenwagen* with dual rear-mounted spares instead of the traditional side-mounts. Some of the best styling on the Model S chassis came from outside Germany. Exotic coachwork from French carrosserie Jacques Saoutchik included a splendid Convertible Coupe; Van Den Plas of Brussels built a Cabriolet, and an even more stylish Cabriolet came from d'Ieteren Frérès in Belgium. The Model S chassis were also fitted with bespoke coachwork in England by Freestone & Webb in traditional British saloon styling, and those delivered to the United States were mounted with coachwork by the Walter M. Murphy Company of Pasadena, California, a firm principally recognized in later years for its work on Model J and SJ Duesenbergs.

Much of the later changes that appeared on the Model S were the work of Dr. Hans Nibel, who had been chief engineer at Benz, and Ferdinand Porsche's successor at Daimler-Benz in January 1929. Porsche had originally gone to work for DMG prior to the merger, and left Daimler-Benz in December 1928. He returned to Austria where he accepted a position as technical director at Steyr. After a year though, he resigned and moved back to Stuttgart where he established a design and engineering firm, Dr. Ing. H.c. F. Porsche GmbH. Throughout the 1930s, Ferdinand Porsche's counsel would be sought by many German automakers, including Daimler-Benz.

Although the Model S was the Mercedes flagship, it wasn't the only popular model offered. Below it, but not too far below, was the all-new 4-liter Straight-Eight Nürburg 460. The 460 chassis measured 145 inches in wheelbase with a narrow 4-foot 9-inch track, and average overall length of 195 inches (16 feet, 3 inches). Suspension was by semielliptic springs with Houdaille shock absorbers, and the 460 offered four-wheel brakes with a vacuum servo system, automatic central chassis lubrication, and a choice of wooden or wire spoke wheels with Rudge hubs.

Powered by a nonsupercharged side-valve straight-eight engine displacing 4,592 cc (80x115 millimeters bore and stroke), the 460 motor developed 90 horsepower[1] at 3,200 rpm, delivered to the rear axle through

a four-speed transmission, available with a choice of two gearbox ratios.

The 460 Nürburg chassis (W 08) were manufactured through 1933, with a total production of 2,893. The pressed-steel drop frame platform was offered in two wheelbase lengths, the standard 3,670-millimeter (145-inch) model and a short 3,430-millimeter (135-inch) Kurz sport version. The 1928–29 Type 460 models were primarily bodied as Limousines, Tourers, or Cabriolets, while a 460 K short wheelbase chassis was available with the same body choices plus a special Sport-Roadster version.

As the 1920s came to a close, Mercedes-Benz launched another magnificent model, the "Grand Mercedes" Type 770. Introduced in 1930, the 7.7-liter passenger cars were the largest, heaviest, and most expensive vehicles to bear the Mercedes name. Available as a touring car, Pullman, sedan, and in several cabriolet versions, the 770 was intended for heads of state and affluent clientele desiring a prestigious, top-flight motorcar. The supercharged 770 developed 150 horsepower normal and a rousing 200 horsepower with the compressor engaged, capable of propelling the enormous 6,000-pound automobiles at a 100-mile per hour clip.

By 1930, Mercedes-Benz had taken a commanding lead in engineering and technology, offering suspension, engine, and transmission designs that were to become the standard of the world within a decade. The greatest prewar achievements in Mercedes-Benz history, however, were yet to come. In the brief period from 1933 to 1939, Daimler-Benz would add another chapter to the story of the automobile.

Further down the price scale from the SS and 460 was the Stuttgart Model 260 offered in the late 1920s. This 10/50-horsepower model features sporty roadster body styling.

CHAPTER FIVE

The 1930s— Mercedes-Benz Sets the Standard

The 500 K and 540 K

The merger of Daimler and Benz brought about an era of momentous advances in automotive design. Between 1930 and 1940, Mercedes-Benz introduced and perfected the four-wheel independent suspension and a supercharged straight-eight that would rival the Model SJ Duesenberg, while at the Sindelfingen Werk, body design advanced beyond that of other European coachbuilders, with the exception of Figoni, Saoutchik, and Chapron, in Paris.

In 1933 Daimler-Benz made yet another stride ahead of its competition with the introduction of a four-wheel, fully independent suspension, fortified by a catalog of sensational coachwork that would soon be known

The 1935 model 500 K Special Sport Roadster pictured is one of the earliest of that body style built by the Sindelfingen factory. Approximately 12 of these true Roadster bodies (those having side curtains rather than roll-up windows) were produced in 1935-36.

The ultimate Mercedes was the SSKL, Super-Sport Kurz-Leicht. The model's list of racing successes includes the German Grand Prix of 1931 with Rudolf Caracciola driving. The six-cylinder 7.1-liter engines had a maximum output of 300 horsepower, the most of any car built at the time. *DaimlerChrysler Classic*

by the name of the city where Daimler first established a factory for the production of aero engines and aircraft during World War I. Sindelfingen was now the factory Karosseriewerk, and since 1919, the design and construction of custom bodies had become its most important role under managing director Hermann Ahrens.

In addition to the Porsche-designed supercharged six-cylinder engines used in the S series, the engineering department developed a new straight-eight, which was introduced in the 1928 Nürburg model. This was also the year Ferdinand Porsche resigned because of differences with the managing board of directors. Nearly a decade after his departure from Daimler-Benz, Porsche would design the Kdf-Wagen, which in no small way resembled the Mercedes-Benz 170 H. Following World War II, the Kdf became the Volkswagen, and the platform upon which Porsche would base the first 356 sports cars in 1948.

In 1930, Daimler-Benz introduced the Grosser Mercedes. The model's imposing appearance made it the vehicle of choice for heads of state, including the Japanese imperial family and Germany's exiled Kaiser Wilhelm II. *DaimlerChrysler Classic*

The next step in D-B AG's conquest of the European market had begun in 1930 with the introduction of a grand luxe model, the magnificent 770 Grosser (7.7 liter) first shown at the Paris Salon. The largest engine in Mercedes-Benz history, it was intended for the great touring cars and limousines being created at the Sindelfingen Werk. The most important design, however, was on a smaller scale, and with half the displacement—the supercharged 3.8-liter straight-eight, with a bore and stroke of 78 x100 millimeters, that would power the most technologically advanced model of the early 1930s, the Type 380.

What few people realize today is that the engineering and styling of the legendary 500 K and 540 K was a by-product of their short-lived predecessor, the Type 380, which was introduced in 1933 and discontinued the following year. Daimler-Benz had already pioneered four-wheel independent suspension with the Type 170, utilizing a transverse leaf spring in the front and a swing axle design with coil springs in the rear. This was refined in 1933 for the Type 380, which became the first production automobile in the world with independent front suspension by means of parallel wishbones and coil springs. The independent rear was a continuation of the proven 170 swing-axle design, but was now fitted with two coil springs per side.

The new front suspension vastly improved ride characteristics by allowing the front wheels to flex slightly to the rear on impact with a bump, further absorbing vibrations before being taken up into the chassis. The shock absorber was a lever-type carried on the outside, behind the spring and attached from the chassis to the top A-arm. In the rear, the revised swing axle design relied on two large coil springs per side, and in back (behind the fuel tank), two horizontal assist springs linking the two axle halves together. In the event one axle was forced up radically, the assist spring would pull the axle down tightly against the pavement. This minimized the swing axle's tendency to tuck up under the car in tight cornering situations, and further

to sport-roadsters, sedans, roadster-coupes, and convertibles in two and two-plus seating, known as the Cabriolet A or Cabriolet B.

The 380's only shortcoming was power, which Daimler-Benz deemed insufficient for the weight of the massive box-section frame, which with coachwork averaged well over two tons. Even with the supercharger engaged (which was only good for short bursts of speed), output was limited to 120 horsepower. A handful of later 1933–1934 models increased output to 140 horsepower and toward the end of production a few delivered 144 horsepower, all at 3,600 rpm. Still, this proved inadequate, except for cars with the lightest-weight open coachwork. The solution was that most favorite of principles adhered to by high-performance devotees on both sides of the Atlantic: "There is no substitute for cubic inches." Thus came the 5.0-liter 500 K.

Considered to be cars of uncommon quality, comfort, and style, the 500 Ks proved their exceptional durability and strength in the Deutschland Fahrt

In the late 1930s the Grosser 770 Mercedes Sedans with compressor were becoming popular with German dignitaries and government leaders. The later 770 models had the same improved suspension as the 540 K and a five-speed gearbox. The long-wheelbase Limousines, such as this 1938 model, were capable of touring at over 100 miles per hour on the Autobahn. *DaimlerChrysler Classic*

improved handling. Similar swing axle designs would be used by Mercedes-Benz for the next 35 years! But in 1933, a car equipped with a four-wheel, coil spring, independent suspension was nothing short of unconventional, considering that most of the automotive world was still relying on solid rear axles and leaf springs.

Thus the 1933–1934 Type 380 introduced virtually all of the features for which its successors are revered, including most of the coachwork. Total production of the 380 (not to be confused with the 380 S, produced in Mannheim in 1932 and 1933) amounted to approximately 157 examples, according to historian Jan Melin, with body styles ranging from open tourers

large box section crossbrace located behind the transmission; and in the rear, two small cross-members that served as front and rear supports for the differential. The frame was tapered at the front, allowing for the narrow radiator, which, along with the engine, was nestled behind the front suspension, (with the exception of short-wheelbase chassis), allowing the frame rails, and therefore the bumpers, to extend well past the grille.

Despite their tremendous weight, the cars could accelerate from a stand to 62 miles per hour (100 kilometers per hour) in under 16 seconds, and in top gear attain a maximum speed of 100 miles per hour. In the 1930s, any automobile that could achieve triple digits was immediately legendary. With the addition of the

Aerodynamics was just beginning to come into vogue in 1933, and in America Cadillac would debut the Fleetwood-bodied V-16 Aero-Dynamic Coupe. At the Berlin show, Mercedes-Benz previewed the 500 K Autobahn-Kurier "Streamline Limousine." By 1935 the company would build a total of four such examples, powered by the new 160-horsepower, 5.0-liter supercharged straight-eight. *DaimlerChrysler Classic*

Among the selection of factory body styles produced at Sindelfingen was the Special Sport Coupe or Sportinnenlenker. The design was first seen on the 500 K chassis in 1935. *DaimlerChrysler Classic*

(roughly "Tour of Germany") endurance tests in 1934. Covering a distance of 2,195.8 kilometers (approximately 1,364 miles) from Baden-Baden, through Stuttgart, Munich, Nuremberg, Dresden, Berlin (Avus), Magdeburg, Cologne, Nürburgring, and Mannheim, and back to Baden-Baden, the factory 500 Ks, along with privately owned Mercedes-Benz entries, virtually dominated a field of more than 190 vehicles.

The 500 K and 540 K were the jewels in the crown of the German motor industry right up to the beginning of World War II. The 500 K and 540 K chassis offered an extraordinary platform upon which to build a custom body. It was composed of two main frame rails, crossbraced by one heavy front I-beam, which supported the radiator and independent front suspension mounting; a smaller bolted-in cross-member, used to support the rear of the engine and transmission; a

5.4-liter 540 K in 1936, the mighty Mercedes had reached its zenith. Producing 115 horsepower, increased to a spirited 180 horsepower with the Roots compressor set in motion, Mercedes-Benz had put to road one of the most powerful production automobiles the world had ever seen.

To take full advantage of the 5.4-liter straight-eight, 540 Ks were equipped with a four-speed manual transmission. First gear was 3.90:1, second 2.28, third 1.45, and top gear 1:1. This was further improved upon in 1939 when 540 K models became available with a new five-speed transmission offering a 0.80:1 overdrive, or *Schnellgang*.

Following the 540 K's introduction, a right-hand-drive model (of which fewer than 200 were built in the 500 K and 540 K series) was reviewed by the editors of Great Britain's prestigious automotive journal *The Motor*.

In the May 11, 1937, issue they put a 540 K Cabriolet to the test and found the mighty new Mercedes ". . . extremely well built throughout, in the characteristic Mercedes-Benz fashion, and the cabriolet coachwork is as robust and as beautifully made as the chassis." Interestingly, before making mention of the car's top speed, the editors were prompt to mention the 540 K's remarkable handling in London traffic. "On the quiet third speed it will amble along at 10 miles per hour with the engine turning a modest 500 rpm. On the same gear the car will accelerate from 10 miles per hour to 70 miles per hour in 19 seconds and will reach 75 miles per hour if the engine is taken a little beyond the recommended limit of 3,500 rpm." At the famed Brooklands racetrack, the test car was pressed to a speed in excess of 90 miles per hour unblown and a rousing 106 miles per hour with the supercharger engaged. Noted *The Motor*, "The latter figure was obtained by timing the Mercedes over a full flying half-mile along the railway straight in complete touring trim with the windshield and foldable head erected." On the open road they discovered the car's excellent balance and handling, even at high speeds. "On a fast main-road bend one can hug the kerb at really high speeds in a way which can only be described as comparable to running on rails."

The 540 K was truly an unparalleled automobile for its time, with an appearance one European journalist in the 1930s described as having "aggressive styling and Teutonic arrogance." Indeed, they were a manifestation of everything Mercedes-Benz had become by the late 1930s, and if these machines of immense strength, power, and presence gave the impression of being pompous or arrogant in their design, it was only because so many other marques paled in comparison. If that was to be construed as "Teutonic arrogance," it was a richly deserved accusation to which Daimler-Benz lent greater substance by dominating European motor racing throughout the 1930s with the incomparable W 25, W 125, W 154, and W 165 Silver Arrows.

As the decade neared an end, the world had turned its full attention toward Germany, not only for its stunning accomplishments in automotive design and grand prix racing but its escalating and unpopular political ideology.

By 1939, when war broke out in Europe, Mercedes-Benz had produced tens of thousands of automobiles, but only 354 500 K chassis from 1934 to 1936 and 406 540 K chassis—97 cars in 1936, 145 in 1937, 95 in 1938, and 69 in 1939. In the overall

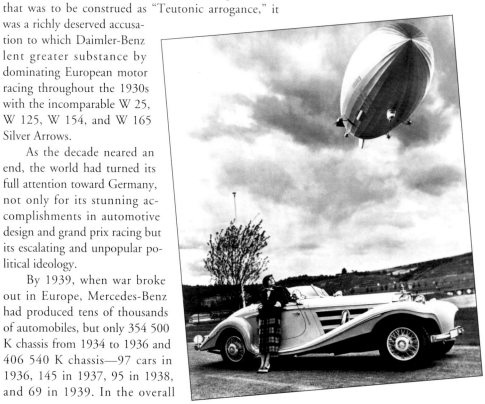

The 500 K and 540 K models measured 5,250 millimeters (206-3/4 inches), from bumper to bumper, on a 3,290-millimeter (129-1/2-inch) standard wheelbase. Track measured 1,515 millimeters (59-5/8 inches) in front and 1,502 millimeters (59-1/8 inches) rear. The 500 K and 540 K chassis could also be ordered in a short K (Kurz) wheelbase of 2,980 millimeters (approx. 117.5 inches). The chassis weight was 1,700 kilograms or 3,750 pounds. This rare photograph of a restored chassis was taken by the author while documenting the restoration of a 540 K Special Coupe.

As a midpriced model, the 55-horsepower Type 230 offered a higher level of styling, as shown in this factory photo of the four-passenger Cabriolet C. Sedan versions of the longer-wheelbase 230 became popular in Germany as taxis because of their high quality and efficient six-cylinder engine. *DaimlerChrysler Classic*

scheme of things, this was an almost inconsequential number of cars, yet their significance on the automotive world was as though production had been tenfold.

Not surprisingly, the production figures are estimates at best, since it is known that some 380s ordered in 1934 were delivered as 500 Ks, while others ordered in 1936 as 500 Ks were fitted with the new 5.4-liter engines, thus becoming 540 Ks! Further confusion comes from the fact that Mercedes-Benz cars were dated by the year in which the chassis was finished. Completed chassis, which were produced in two wheelbase lengths, 2,980 millimeters (117 inch) and 3,290 millimeters (129-1/2 inch), sometimes sat at Untertürkheim for up to two years before being fitted with coachwork. A total of 20 540 K sedans with special armor and bulletproof glass, were assembled during 1942 for the "Aktion P" series, built for military use, along with 770 Grosser Mercedes staff cars and G 4 half-tracks.

Aside from a handful of one-off customs, the Sindelfingen Werk designed and produced nearly all the coachwork for the 500 K and 540 K series. According to Jan Melin's in-depth research of factory records published in his 1985 book *Mercedes-Benz—The Supercharged 8-Cylinder Cars of the 1930s*, there were over a dozen body types produced; the Limousine, also called an Innenlenker or Saloon; the formal Pullman-Limousine; the Spezial-Coupé; Kombinations-Coupé (a convertible coupe with optional removable hardtop); the Autobahn-Kurier or Stromlinien-Limousine; a Normal-Roadster, sometimes referred to as Sport-Roadster; the Spezial-Roadster, distinguished by its concealed top, metal boot, and divided "V" windshield; Special Coupé (hardtop version of the Spezial Roadster); Offener Tourenwagen (open tourer or phaeton); and a series of Cabriolets: A, B, C, D, and F, the latter two being exceptionally rare. The factory also produced one-off special orders. In many cases, Mercedes-Benz itself gave the same body style two or even three different names over the years.

A small number of 500 K and 540 K chassis were delivered to outside coachbuilders, predominantly Erdmann & Rossi, which was responsible for producing several exceptional body designs, including the 500 K Stromlinien (streamlined) Limousine and Roadster, and the distinctively styled Sport Cabriolet. Most of the coachwork produced at the Berlin-Halensee karosseriewerk was for Mercedes-Benz. More than 220 cars were bodied between 1926 and 1939, most of which were commissioned by the Daimler-Benz factory. A variety of roadster, cabriolet, phaeton, and limousine coachwork was provided for Daimler-Benz, with approximately 21 500 K and from 8 to 12 540 K bodies bearing the Erdmann & Rossi-Jos. Neuss emblem.

During the 1920s and 1930s, Erdmann & Rossi designs lent an air of sportiness to Mercedes-Benz, as well as to Maybach, Bentley, Rolls-Royce, and Horch models. With only a few exceptions, such as the 540 K Special Roadster, Special Coupe, extremely rare Kombinations-Coupe, and the Autobahn-Kurier, all of which were designed at Sindelfingen, Erdmann & Rossi body styles were vastly more progressive. Among Erdmann & Rossi's most prominent styling cues were double-frame "V" windshields, rear-mounted spares, and bold, horizontal hood vents, each accented with a raised chromed spear that served as a handle to open and close the louver. These specific features, either individually or

in combination, appeared on Mercedes-Benz chassis bodied throughout the 1930s. The most popular Erdmann & Rossi body style was the Sport Cabriolet, of which 18 were built for the 500 K and 540 K chassis, plus an additional 17 for the 2.9-liter Mercedes-Benz, and a single example on the 3.8-liter chassis.

Mercedes-Benz was the first automaker to put a diesel passenger car into production. The 260 D made its debut in 1936. *DaimlerChrysler Classic*

Although it would be difficult to refer to any 540 K as anything less than stunning, some were more so than others. The Special Coupe and Special Roadster, rarity notwithstanding, were two of the most striking, if not *the* most striking, of all Sindelfingen designs. If the 540 K was conceived for the purpose of making a statement, the Special Roadsters were the last word. Introduced at the 1936 Berlin Auto Show, which conveniently coincided with the 50th anniversary of the Benz Patent-Motorwagen, the 540 K Special Roadster was the most expensive Mercedes-Benz model offered. In all, there were six variations dubbed Special Roadster by Daimler-Benz, beginning with the 1933 Type 380 and progressing through the 500 K and 540 K, each becoming gradually more sophisticated.

A design that many historians believe to be the most beautiful ever to grace an automobile chassis, the Special Roadster was an exercise in no-compromise styling. Passenger capacity of this huge car was two

(plus two in the rumble seat). Among the many features that exemplified 540 K Special Roadster styling was the use of chromium embellishments along the length of the fenders, hood, doors, and rear deck. These, and the chromed handles for doors, hood, and rumble seat, were all special castings. Another unique feature was the sharply angled vee-windscreen. Spotlights on either side of the frame were also specially made for the cars, each with a convex mirror attached to the back of its housing, serving as the only means for the driver to see alongside or to the rear. The 540 K Special Roadster was also the first Mercedes-Benz to offer silver metallic paint, known at Daimler-Benz as "fisch-silber grau," and was the first to enjoy a completely disappearing convertible top, stowed beneath a metal lid. The interior was also atypical, highlighted by a steering wheel, gearshift knob, emergency brake handle, and reserve fuel knob all in white. Instruments for the 540 K had the appearance of a hand-made Swiss timepiece, and were usually surrounded by a mother-of-pearl fascia, adding the final touch of elegance to the car's luxuriously appointed interior.

At the other end of the spectrum, both in terms of price and performance, was another model introduced in 1936, the 260 D—the world's first diesel production car, which was built at Sindelfingen. Benz had been the first to delve into diesel manufacturing before the merger. At Daimler-Benz, efforts were redoubled and the 260 D was the fruit of that labor. From 1936 to the present day, Mercedes has been the world leader in diesel design, engineering, and production, having built more than three and a half million diesel automobiles in the past 65 years.

Not every great car with the Mercedes name was expensive. The lower-priced series, such as the 290, was far more important to the company's continued existence than the 540 K. With an inline six-cylinder engine, the 290 was never intended to be as flamboyant as the more costly eight-cylinder supercharged cars, yet they too were often fitted with exceptional coachwork. For the period, the 290 was an evolutionary model, incorporating advanced designs, such as a dropped-box section frame with four-wheel fully independent suspension, overdrive gearbox, divided track rod steering, hydraulic brakes, and one-shot lubrication.

Most 290 bodies were traditional and rather ordinary, distinguished mainly by the Mercedes-Benz grille and star. The few exceptions were the Streamlined Saloon, Roadster, and Cabriolets. One book on Mercedes-Benz catalogs 25 different body styles on the 290's 2,880-millimeter (113-inch) Kurz (short) chassis and 3,300-millimeter (130-inch) long chassis.

While nearly all of the 290s built were assembled at the Mannheim Werk and bore the Mannheim emblem just forward of the driver door, a handful of special orders were bodied by Sindelfingen—a 1935 Cabriolet A, 1936 Roadster, and certain long-wheelbase versions of the 1934–1937 Cabriolet B and Cabriolet D. Additionally, a short-wheelbase 290 Sport Cabriolet was built in 1934 by Karosserie Papler, and Cabriolet D and F long-wheelbase models by Erdmann & Rossi, in 1935–1937. The average price of a luxury 290 model was exactly half that of a 540 K.

The total of 290s built between 1933 and 1937 was 8,214, still hardly mass production. In comparison, Mercedes-Benz turned out more than 39,000 of the popular and affordable 170 and 170V models during the same period. If one were to overlook that the car's best effort

in top gear barely exceeded 100 kilometers per hour, or that it took better than 30 seconds to get there, if one had the marks equivalent to $1,250, a Mercedes-Benz could be purchased. At that price even the guy flipping schnitzels on the corner could afford to own one.

Cars like the 170V were the bread-and-butter models. A total of 10 cataloged body styles were offered from 1936 through 1942, with production totaling more than 70,000 units before the war ended commercial automobile manufacturing. The original series was introduced in 1931 in response to the stumbling European economy that had arrived on the threadbare coattails of the 1929 stock market crash, a financial calamity that had not only staggered the U.S. economy but denied Europe one of its most lucrative export markets.

Intended as a conservative offering, the 170 nonetheless blazed some technological trails, offering features not available from other European car companies. For a base price equivalent to $1,000, the 170 came with a responsive 1.7-liter, six-cylinder engine,

The design of the rear-engined 170 H continued to improve and by 1936 appeared in this very recognizable form. At virtually the same time the 170 H was being designed, Ferdinand Porsche was working on the Kdf prototypes for Hitler, with the final version of the car first appearing in 1938, two years after this Mercedes 170 H. *DaimlerChrysler Classic*

Mercedes luxury came in many price ranges during the 1930s, and this stylish Cabriolet A body was offered on the midpriced Type 370 S Mannheim chassis.

With its robust and ambitious engineering (X-type oval-tube frame, independent front suspension, transverse spring rear swing axle, L-head four-cylinder engine, and four-speed gearbox) the Mercedes-Benz 170 V went into production at the end of 1935 as a 1936 model to replace the earlier 170 series.

The 370 S was the top sports model built between 1929 and 1934. The "S" in the name denotes special design, for which chief designer Hans Nibel chose a very pronounced drop center frame in order to have a lower center of gravity and improve handling.

Economies of scale dictated that Mercedes-Benz offer more inexpensive cars during the 1930s. Very near the bottom of the product line was the boxy little Type 170 Innenlenker (Sedan). The small car offered big car features, however, including independent suspension, overdrive transmission, and four-wheel hydraulic brakes. What it lacked was styling . . .

. . . which Daimler-Benz provided with the second generation 170V, a new line of small cars offering better performance, greater fuel economy, and sporty styling, as evidenced by this 1937 Cabriolet A. *DaimlerChrysler Classic*

The 770 was the largest car ever produced by Mercedes-Benz. Most 770s were purchased for royal families or used by government officials, such as this 1931 model built for the exiled Kaiser Wilhelm II. Note crest of the Hohenzollerns in place of the Mercedes star on the radiator.

Although it would be difficult to refer to any 540 K as anything less than stunning, the 540 K Special Coupe was one of the most striking of all Sindelfingen designs. It managed as no other 540 K had, to blend the sweeping fenderlines and tapered rear deck of the sporty Special Roadster with the refined elegance and style of a closed coupe—a feat attempted by numerous automakers throughout the 1930s, but never executed as beautifully as the 540 K Special Coupes.

TOP LEFT, PREVIOUS PAGE:
The rarest of all Sindelfingen-built models, the Autobahn-Kurier was the most dynamically styled car to emerge from the German styling studio. The sporty fastback design was contemporary to models shown by Packard and Cadillac in the late 1930s, which shared a similar configuration. This is a 1939 540 K version and the most beautifully styled of the series.

PREVIOUS PAGE:
The Germans have always had their own, often unique, interpretations of certain words, and the Special Roadster was one such case. A Roadster, as defined by Daimler-Benz, was a car that had no padded headliner in the convertible top, which could either fold down very low or be completely concealed. Lowering the top on a typical Mercedes-Benz Cabriolet left a stack of fabric, bows, and headliner high enough to obscure the rear view. The Special Roadster did away with this completely by concealing the folded top underneath a solid boot. Special Roadsters were also built with open stacked rear deck-mounted spares, or concealed spares as shown. The latter was always considered to be the most stylish. *Photos by Dennis Adler from the Bud Lyon collection*

four-wheel fully independent suspension, central lubrication, four-wheel hydraulic brakes, pressed steel wheels, and an antitheft steering wheel lock. While any one of these features might have been found on competitive automobiles, no other European car of that day offered all of them at anything like the 170's price. Originally there were only two body styles available: a four-door Sedan and the more spacious Cabriolet C. A Roadster and Cabriolet A were added in 1932 and a two-door Phaeton in 1934.

Although they sold well, early 170 styling lacked somewhat in eye appeal, especially when parked alongside a 290 or a 500 K. Even the lines of the sporty two-seat 170 Roadster were square and stodgy, so in 1936 Daimler-Benz stylists gave the model line a new, more daring look with the 170 V. Now even the most affordable Mercedes was a tony looking automobile.

To improve structural design and ride quality, a new tubular backbone frame replaced the original box-section chassis. The 170V was also noticeably longer than its predecessor, riding on a 2,845-millimeter (113.8-inch) wheelbase versus the 170's 2,600-millimeter (104-inch) platform.

The greatest change, however, lay beneath the hood, where a more efficient four-cylinder engine replaced the 170's six-cylinder motor! It was a case of less being more. In comparison, the 170V displaced 1,697 cc, with a bore and stroke of 73.5x100 millimeters and output of 38 horsepower at 3,400 rpm, whereas the old six with a 1,692-cc displacement and 65x85-millimeter bore and stroke delivered only 32 horsepower. Top speed was improved as well, from a maximum of 90 kilometers per hour (56 miles per hour) to a top end of 108 kilometers per hour (67 miles per hour). A new transmission completed the mechanical revisions, with a four-speed manual replacing the 170's three-speed gearing.

The most attractive new 170V bodies were the Cabriolet A and Roadster. Both were two-seat designs,

The Mercedes That Mercedes Didn't Build

The automobile, both here and abroad, has become one of modern man's preeminent obsessions, one of the few objects that we assume to be extensions of our own personality. Like a bespoke suit or a lavish home, an automobile makes a statement about its owner. In the early years of the automotive trade, it also made a statement about its builder. The cars of Wilhelm and Karl Maybach spoke volumes about their creators. They were in spirit, if not in intent, extensions of the Mercedes, cars that could have been built by Daimler had events in the early 1900s taken a different course.

Following his departure from DMG, Wilhelm Maybach joined Zeppelin, and along with his son Karl, also a gifted engineer, established his own company to build aero engines. Once again war would alter the course of history. After World War I, Maybach's design and manufacturing of motorcars wasn't so much an expansion of the company as it was a necessity for its survival. As a condition in the Treaty of Versailles, German manufacturers were forbidden to produce aircraft and aircraft engines in the early years following World War I, which left the Maybachs with little to do, so in 1921 the plant in Friedrichshafen began to produce automobiles under the name Maybach Motoren-Werken. The first, the Model W 3, was introduced that year powered by a Maybach 70-horsepower straight six and a two-speed transmission. The new automobiles were actually the work of Maybach's son, Karl, but in the background, the father, the teacher, Wilhelm was always present. The W 3 was followed in 1926 with the new 120-horsepower W 5, and in 1928 by a modified version of the same car cataloged as the W 5 SG.

While Mercedes were regarded as very stylish automobiles, the majority of Maybach body designs were conservative in nature, like the company's humble Swabian founder. The six-cylinder models were primarily bodied as Limousines, Pullman-Cabriolets (phaetons), Sports Cabriolets (Convertible Coupes), and four-door Cabriolets (Convertible Sedans), most of which were supplied by Karosseriewerk Hermann Spohn in Ravensburg. Selling for an average of 31,500 to 35,000 marks, the cars were competitive to those built by Mercedes-Benz and were "in revenge," one might say, for the shoddy treatment Wilhelm Maybach had received from the DMG board in the early 1900s. Then, too, there must have been some satisfaction in seeing Daimler forced into a merger with competitor Benz & Cie. in 1926, in order to guarantee the company's future in the recession-torn post–World War I years. Of course, this merger only served to strengthen both Daimler and Benz, forcing Maybach to build an even better car.

This new model arrived in 1929, the same year that the *Graf Zeppelin* circled the world in 448 hours. The mighty airship had been powered by five 550-horsepower Mayback V-12 engines. Following the August flight, Maybach introduced the company's first V-12 automobile, a car intended to outclass the finest Mercedes-Benz and compete in the luxury market against such lofty makes as Rolls-Royce and Hispano-Suiza.

The 1929 12-cylinder DS marked the high point of Maybach's career, and sadly it was his last. Wilhelm Maybach passed away on December 29, at age 83, but not before his son had paid him tribute by building a car that even Daimler-Benz could not offer its customers. In his last days he must have taken comfort in the knowledge that through Karl, Maybach had in some small way triumphed over those who had driven him from DMG. He was buried in the Uff cemetery in Cannstatt where his friend, Gottlieb Daimler, had been laid to rest almost 30 years before.

For the great German automakers, 1929 was a year in which not only Wilhelm Maybach breathed his last, but so too, Karl Benz, and the Baroness von Wiegel, once a young girl named Mercedes Jellinek.

Karl Maybach followed the 1929 "12" with the 150-horsepower, 7-liter, 60-degree V-12 DS 7 (Double Six Cylinders, 7 Liters) Zeppelin model in 1930. The high-torque 12 had a bore of 86 millimeters and a stroke of 100 millimeters, delivering peak horsepower at just 2,800 rpm. In 1931 an even more powerful 8-liter version was introduced with a bore and stroke of 92x100 millimeters, delivering a robust 200 horsepower at 3,200 rpm.

The first V-12s utilized a conventional Maybach three-speed with an overdrive unit from the W 5 SG that allowed six forward speeds. The pneumatically-operated OD was actuated via a control on the steering wheel hub. The DS 8 was equipped with a new five-speed gearbox with a direct drive on top. Once more to move ahead of Mercedes, in 1938 Maybach introduced a new seven-speed gearbox! This new version had an extremely low first gear, a 1:1 sixth gear, and a 0.77:1 overdrive. The most successful design was the Maybach five-speed, known as the Doppelschnellgang (double overdrive), which offered two drive ranges, low and normal. The extra low gear, with a 4.50:1 ratio, was only used on steep grades. The first gear, with a 1:3 ratio, was considered the normal starting-out gear, with the change up effected via two levers on the steering wheel hub. The system was pneumatically operated, and to select a gear the driver moved the levers to the correct combination for each desired speed, lifted off the gas momentarily, allowing the gear to be engaged, and depressed the throttle again. It was in effect a form of preselector similar to the French Cotal, but required no declutching to activate. The seven-speed introduced on the 1937 DS 8 was an even more ingenious design, which allowed gear selection via a single lever on the steering column, graduated from N for neutral through top gear, an overdrive that was ostensibly an eighth gear. Forward and reverse were selected by a floor-mounted lever, so it was theoretically possible to have eight speeds in reverse!

The luxuriant Maybach Zeppelin DS 8 was far more elegant than the Mercedes-Benz 770. It was also substantially larger. Despite its massive size, the Maybach was capable of attaining 100-miles per hour with most coachwork.

The bare chassis in U.S. dollars commanded a price in 1934 of $8,000—roughly the same as a Model J Duesenberg chassis cost in the United States. Maybach chassis were available in two wheelbase lengths, 144 inches and 147 inches, the former being discontinued in 1937.

The DS 8 line was produced through 1940, endowing Maybach with a reputation that ultimately came closer to that of Rolls-Royce than Mercedes-Benz. The Maybach Zeppelins came to be regarded as one of Germany's leading high status luxury cars.

Always of very conservative design, Maybach Twelve Limousines and Cabriolets appealed to the very wealthy, the German aristocracy who found Sindelfingen's styling for the Mercedes-Benz perhaps too flamboyant, and the Auto Union's luxurious Horch line too middle class. Maybach also produced a companion line of six-cylinder models that culminated in the 1935 SW, the most popular of all Maybachs.

In all, the company produced around 2,200 cars of 13 different models built between 1921 and 1941, two decades of remarkable automobiles created by the Maybach father and son, cars that had things gone differently could have been Mercedes.

With the outbreak of a second war in Europe, Maybach began production of 12-cylinder diesel

Approximately 300 Maybach Zeppelins were produced between 1930 and 1939. This example from the Nethercutt Collection was built in 1932 and bodied by Karosserie Spohn in Ravensburg as a four-door Cabriolet (Convertible Sedan). It was originally sold for $12,000, with the coachwork having made up about $4,000 of that price. Believed to have been registered to the Aviation Ministry in Berlin, the car was discovered behind the Iron Curtain in the late 1960s. After some difficulty with permits, the Polish Ministry of Finance, and the Bureau of Customs, the rare Maybach Zeppelin was brought out of Poland in the fall of 1969 by Leonard Potter, who sold it that December to J. B. Nethercutt. Documentation had traced the car back to three previous owners, Tadeusz Tabenski of Warsaw, Poland; English diplomat George Korzeniowsi; and to the German Aviation Ministry.

engines for use in tanks and half-track vehicles. After the war, the company continued to manufacture diesels. Unfortunately, the era for Maybach automobiles was over, even though the factory briefly entertained the idea in the early 1950s. In 1960, Maybach Motorenbau GmbH and Daimler-Benz AG entered into an agreement whereby Maybach would produce Mercedes-Benz diesel engines. Today, the company is part of the DaimlerChrysler Group, producing Mercedes-Benz heavy diesel engines at Friedrichshafen, under the name Motoren-Turbinen-Union (MTU).

One can easily draw the conclusion that Mercedes-Benz owns the Maybach name. Thus the new Twelve-Cylinder Maybach luxury car, which may well see the light of day in the twenty-first century, will bring full circle the legacy of Gottlieb Daimler and Wilhelm Maybach. They will, in a sense, be together again, if only in name.

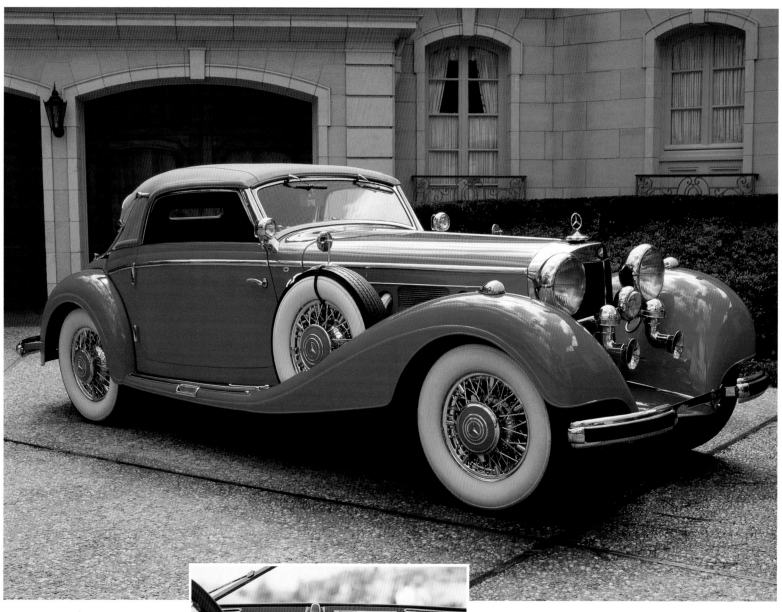

Variations on a theme. A 540 K Cabriolet A was still a sporty looking car, though less dramatic than a special roadster *Jerry J. Moore collection.*

The 540 K interiors changed over the years. From the very elegant look of the 1937 dashboard with its fine jewel-like gauges, to the more contemporary look of this late 1939 model (one of the last built before the war) featuring an entirely new style of instruments, dash fascia, and the addition of a dashboard-mounted radio!

The Sport Cabriolet, created by Karosserie Erdmann & Rossi of Berlin, combined the best attributes of a Special Roadster and Cabriolet A to create a 4- or 5-passenger model unlike any other. Among Erdmann & Rossi's most prominent styling cues were double-frame vee windshields, rear-mounted spares, and bold, horizontal hood vents, each accented with a raised chromed spear, which served as a handle to open and close the louver. Despite being a 4- or 5-seat design with blind rear quarter, technically a Cabriolet C, the Sport Cabriolet was so distinctively different in appearance from other Cabriolet C designs that Erdmann & Rossi virtually created a new version. A Cabriolet C was generally tall with the top raised, and somewhat formal in appearance, with a slightly raked, flat windshield, dual side mounts, and a flat or curved trunk lid. Hardly a description that fits this 1937 Erdmann & Rossi Cabriolet.

although the Roadster allowed a second couple to squeeze together in the narrow rumble seat. The Cabriolet had the traditional fabric stack and folded landau irons when the top was lowered, but the Roadster's cleverly designed top collapsed backward, and then swiveled down behind the seats. The completely concealed top allowed the driver an unobstructed rear view and lent new sophistication to the affordable little roadster's profile.

More than a high water mark for Mercedes-Benz, the 170V was also the foundation for the company's revival after World War II. The 170V Sedan was the first postwar Mercedes, basically a 1942 model reintroduced in 1947. Regrettably, nothing remotely like the sporty 170V Rumble Seat Roadster would reappear until the 1950s.

At the same time traditional models like the 170V, 230, 260 D, 290, and 370 Mannheim were being produced, Daimler-Benz turned its attention toward an even lower-priced line, with the innovative rear-engine Type 130, 150 H and later 170 H, a car which by no small coincidence would foreshadow another soon-to-be popularized German model, the Volkswagen.

As the conflagration being fanned by Hitler and Mussolini in 1939 ensured that all of Europe would be at war before year's end, the greatest era in Mercedes-Benz history was coming to a close. In the aftermath of six war-torn years, it would take more than a decade for the company to rebuild its factories and its image as a leader in automotive design and engineering. Many German automakers would not survive at all, casualties of war on an industrial scale, one that would very nearly claim Mercedes as well.

CHAPTER SIX

Mercedes-Benz in the 1950s

Postwar Reconstruction—Old World Cars for a New World

The bombs stopped falling over Berlin. When the sounds of tanks, planes, and M1 Garands finally fell silent on May 8, 1945, Europe's leading automotive manufacturers were surrounded by rubble. Mostly their own. In Germany, Allied bombers had targeted the Daimler-Benz, BMW, and the once all-conquering Auto Union factories. And accurately. In the surrounding areas, houses remained standing, but the Daimler-Benz Werk in Mannheim, Sindelfingen, Gaggenau near Baden-Baden, and Untertürkheim were nearly leveled to their foundations, and most of the tooling and machinery within badly damaged or destroyed. When Daimler-Benz managers returned to the sites under authority of the Allied Occupation Forces, they were met by what appeared to be the total devastation of their company. Mercedes-Benz

The models intended for more affluent buyers, particularly those in the United States, were the 300 S and Sc series, which were virtually hand-built and commensurately priced at upward of $12,000.

Few words could describe what remained of Daimler-Benz after World War II. The main factories in Mannheim, Sindelfingen, and Untertürkheim had been bombed. What remained was rubble atop machinery, twisted steel, and offices that, a few years earlier, had produced the greatest automobiles Europe had ever known. *DaimlerChrysler Classic*

This most bizarre Type 170 Sedan was built in the early years of the war. With fuel shortages, a number of cars were converted to use a wood-gas generator. The modified engines produced only 22 horsepower, but there was no shortage of wood in the forests and a full tank of lumber was good for 100 kilometers between fill-ups. *DaimlerChrysler Classic*

would have to be resurrected, quite literally, from its own still smoldering ashes.

Germany was more than a defeated country—it was a devastated country, its historic architecture laid waste and its industry at a standstill. Its people, its good people—civilians, workers, men, women, and children—who had nothing to do with the horrid history of the Third Reich, had been left with virtually no economy and a nation divided into east and west. The British, American, and Russian military jointly occupied the country, the Soviets having laid claim to the eastern sector with half of Berlin now in the Russian zone. In the face of this, Daimler-Benz began to rebuild in May 1945.

As renowned historian Beverly Rae Kimes noted in her 1986 book, *The Star and the Laurel,* "What happened at Daimler-Benz was on one hand relatively simple and on the other unbelievably complicated and ironic. Daimler-Benz products were as much a part of the German war effort as GM, Ford, and Chrysler products were of the American or Rolls-Royce aircraft engines were of the British." Mercedes-Benz just happened to be on the losing side. It was manufacturing the V-12, fuel-injected, turbocharged engines used in practically every important Luftwaffe plane, and building a variety of military vehicles ranging from staff cars and half-tracks to trucks and tanks. Pretty much what Ford, GM, and Chrysler were doing in the United States. Had the war continued on into the late 1940s, and had Germany completed deployment of jet fighters and bombers, which were being built with engines designed and manufactured by BMW, planes that could have swayed the balance of power had they been ready any sooner than 1944, who is to say that at some point in a more protracted conflict Germany wouldn't have bombed Detroit? To the Allied forces, Germany's auto industry had been a target, and Mercedes-Benz was the largest on the map.

The Nazis had insinuated themselves within the company through Jakob Werlin, (the "house Nazi" as Kimes dubbed him), and as an advisor to Hitler his power at D-B AG was irrefutable. Those managers who failed to comply, or had opinions that differed from those of the Third Reich, such as Daimler-Benz supervisory board member and Deutsche Bank director Hermann Köhler, were arrested, tried, convicted, and executed. Others, who had Jewish relatives, were forced out of the company, if they were lucky. Similar

The postwar reconstruction of Daimler-Benz was built on the back of the 170V, about the only car for which tooling remained intact. The first postwar production cars were introduced in 1947, and were, for all intents, 1942 models. Within two years the rebuilt assembly lines were producing 170 models equipped with either a four-cylinder gasoline engine or a new 1.7-liter diesel. *DaimlerChrysler Classic*

Mercedes-Benz would have to be resurrected from its own still-smoldering ashes, and by 1949 much of the work had been done, as evidenced in this factory photo showing the new 170V assembly lines in Untertürkheim. *DaimlerChrysler Classic*

By 1951, Mercedes-Benz was well on its way to becoming a full-line manufacturer once again. *DaimlerChrysler Classic*

events were taking place at BMW, which was second only to Mercedes-Benz in the German war effort. Franz Josef Popp, chairman of the Bayerische Motoren Werke, was forced to resign under threat of internment in a concentration camp. The Nazis put their own man in charge. So neither firm really had control over events, and this is something most people need to be reminded of even a half-century later.

In the aftermath of the war, the Americans allowed Mercedes-Benz employees to return to work at Untertürkheim and begin reconstruction in May 1945. It started with the repair and manufacturing of the Type 170, the only model for which tooling still remained intact. By 1948 over 6,000 of the prewar 170s had been assembled, and within five years from the day employees returned to the bombed out ruins of their company, Daimler-Benz would have its assembly lines and factories rebuilt. In 1952, Germany's premier automaker would once again leave the automotive world utterly amazed, and at a time when something amazing was least expected from Mercedes.

Germany had been divided into two countries, the new West German Federal Republic, and East Germany, which was controlled by the Soviets. Fortunately for Daimler-Benz they were on the right side of the division.

Every age had a superlative automobile. In the 1950s it was the Mercedes-Benz 300. Often modified, technically as well as aesthetically, it remained in production for a remarkable 11 years. Pictured is a 300b Cabriolet D built in 1954. *DaimlerChrysler Classic*

The same could not be said for BMW, which had lost all of its major manufacturing facilities in Eisenach to the Russians. It would take years before BMW was able to rebuild itself.

After starting out servicing American military trucks and repairing 170s in 1946, the first postwar Mercedes production cars were built at Untertürkheim in 1947. They were, for all intents and purposes, 1942 models, but within two years, the rebuilt assembly lines were producing 170s equipped with either a four-cylinder gasoline engine or a new 1.7-liter, pushrod overhead valve diesel, developing 38 horsepower at 3,200 rpm. With fuel in short supply, the diesel was an immediate success. An improved 170 Da was introduced in May 1950, with production running through April 1952. The 170 Da was slightly more powerful, having a larger displacement of 1.77 liters and an output of 40

horsepower. The 170 Da was followed by the Db model, which offered a wider track, hypoid rear axle, a slightly revised hoodline, and a larger windshield. This version was continued until October 1953. The final series, beginning with the 170 DS, was built concurrently with the 170 Da and 170 Db, from January 1952 until August 1953. The very last version, the 170S-D was produced from July 1953 until September 1955, when the entire 170 series, both the diesel and the 170 V through 170 Vb gasoline models was retired, as were their old prewar body styles. By 1953, Mercedes-Benz had reestablished itself as one of the world's leading automakers, and it had accomplished this feat in only seven years!

If there was one significant feature distinguishing American cars built in the early 1950s from those produced in Europe during the same period, it was styling. Designers in America were experimenting with new ideas, trying to break away from the prewar look, which had seemingly been held in a state of suspended animation until the early 1950s. Throughout much of Europe, and Germany in particular, the battlefield had extended right up to the front door of the world's oldest and most established automakers, leaving them little choice but to pick up the pieces of a broken industry and start from scratch; but unlike American stylists who tossed everything out the window and started over in the 1950s, the Europeans began with a clean sheet of paper that still had tracing lines put down in the late 1930s. The result was a brief generation of cars whose styling aesthetically integrated the classic bodylines of the past with the contemporary look of the future.

The 300 SL was a masterpiece that sprang full born from the imagination of Rudolf Uhlenhaut, Fritz Nallinger, and Karl Wiffert in 1951. Using essentially off-the-shelf parts, they created a tubular space frame to support the engine and suspension, taken from the production 300 model, and then surrounded it with an aerodynamic sports car body that rewrote the book on automobile design. This 1952 racing prototype provided for sensation after sensation the next year in sports car and rally races, driven at various times by Hermann Lang, Karl Kling, and Fritz Reiss. *DaimlerChrysler Classic*

the elimination of traditions, that decision was pivotal and has not since been violated. A Mercedes-Benz is still unmistakably a Mercedes-Benz.

The road that would lead to new prosperity was a difficult one. Daimler-Benz, like all German automakers, and Germany itself, was under the watchful eye of a mistrusting world. Mercedes-Benz still bore the stain of the Third Reich. Almost every photograph surfacing of Hitler and his generals showed them riding in a Mercedes, and throughout the early postwar years it looked as if Mercedes-Benz would never be able to disassociate itself with that image. Then something miraculous happened. The 300 Series.

The new Type 300 and companion 220 series were the first Daimler-Benz automobiles to carry entirely new postwar styling, with a more streamlined, envelope-type body incorporating the headlamps into the front fenders. The Type 300 was also the first Mercedes

It was one of Mercedes' greatest triumphs, the 1955 victory by Stirling Moss and Denis Jenkinson in the Mille Miglia. Pictured left to right, Daimler-Benz Manager Ludwig Krauss, Design Director Rudolf Uhlenhaut, Jenkinson, Moss, and Daimler-Benz Director Hans Scherenberg.
DaimlerChrysler Classic

The gestation of the 300 SL showing a 1952 race car at right and, moving left, an early preproduction prototype, a 1954 300 SL Coupe, and the stunning 300 SLR Competition Coupe built for Rudolf Uhlenhaut in 1955.
DaimlerChrysler Classic

At Daimler-Benz, this set of guidelines brought about one of the most exciting periods in the company's history. Dr. Wilhelm Haspel, who had returned as company director in January 1948, had instructed body engineer Karl Wilfert and his staff to ensure that the traditional, upright Mercedes radiator motif remain an integral part of the all-new range of cars being planned for the early 1950s. In an era when *all new* often meant

designed with the American market in mind, a market 20 million deep and clamoring for anything new. Suddenly, here was a car so beautiful that it eclipsed the Nazi stigma that had clung to the earlier postwar Mercedes.

Coachwork for the Type 300 series was produced at the Daimler-Benz factory in Sindelfingen and was first available in two body styles, a slim-pillar four-door

Sedan and a pillarless four-door Convertible. The 300 series, like the smaller 220 series, looked modern, yet quintessentially Mercedes. In Europe the popularity of the 300 grew rapidly and in the new Germany it became the high-status motorcar of the 1950s. The 300 Sedans became the choice of foreign embassies, dignitaries, and heads of state. In Germany it was even referred to popularly as the "Adenauer-Wagen" after new West German Chancellor Konrad Adenauer, one of many prominent political figures who chose the 300 for personal transportation.

Referred to in German as a Limousine 4 Türen, the 300's design concept was ultraconservative, a quite successful attempt to produce a prestige German motorcar that would garner the same esteem as a Rolls-Royce. Notes retired Daimler-Benz design director Bruno Sacco: "When you consider that this car concept was continually being improved and rolled off the assembly lines in Sindelfingen until 1962, you will conclude that the clientele was happy with it."

In its overall design the Type 300 was a tremendously impressive car, particularly the four-door Convertible Sedan. In America the 300 Series was virtually in a class by itself, with the exception of the latest Rolls-Royce models. Even Cadillac, the unrivaled American standard of luxury, could not compare with the Mercedes, at least in the minds of those who chose the exclusivity of imported makes over Detroit's latest.

One of the longest running models in the company's history, the 300 series had an 11-year production life. The first series Sedan was built from late 1951 through March 1954, with regular production of the four-door Convertible beginning in April 1952. The original 300 models were succeeded by the 300b, barely externally unchanged, but delivering 10 more horsepower and equipped with larger brakes. Although

The 300 SL Roadster's predecessor and successor was the 190 SL introduced in 1954 and produced through 1963. More than 25,000 were built. The 190 SL Roadster was the ideal affordable sports car, with a 105-horsepower four-cylinder engine and the option of a removable hardtop for all-weather driving. *DaimlerChrysler Classic*

popular, production figures were never high—approximately 6,200 Sedans and a negligible 591 Convertibles in both series, through the summer of 1955. The 300c was introduced in September 1955 and produced through July 1957. Daimler-Benz built 1,430 300c Sedans and 51 Convertibles. The last in the series, the 300d, were assembled on a longer 124-inch wheelbase (versus the original 120-inch span). The body was updated with a flatter, more squared-up roofline, longer rear fenders, and a slightly wider grille. And, in keeping with contemporary styling, the d-series Sedan lost its fixed center pillars to become a true four-door hard-top. Mechanical fuel injection was also adopted, along with a higher compression ratio, increasing output to 160 horsepower. Offered from late 1957 through early 1962, nearly 3,100 hardtops and 65 Convertibles were produced in this series.

The 300 was the largest and fastest automobile yet introduced in postwar Germany, and the car's success in the home market was matched by its popularity and celebrity both in America and throughout Europe. Owners included legendary American architect Frank Lloyd Wright, film stars Gary Cooper, Bing Crosby, and Yul Brynner. The 300 also became the state car for Ethiopian ruler Haile Selassie, India's Jawaharlal Nehru, the Shah of Iran, and King Gustav of Sweden. Even British military hero Field Marshal Montgomery, who had seen more than his fair share of Mercedes-Benz vehicles during World War II, gave in to the allure of the 300.

Although total production figures may not have been remarkable, 11,430 examples built over an 11-year span, the real value was in reestablishing the luxury image Mercedes-Benz had created in the 1920s and 1930s. The 300 Series accomplished this feat in a manner unparalleled by any automobile produced in the last 50 years.

With the sportier Type 300 S and its immediate successor, the 300 Sc model, Mercedes reawakened emotions in automotive enthusiasts that had lain dormant since the 540 K stirred their souls in the 1930s. The new cars were a perfect marriage of hand-crafted old world coachwork, classically inspired styling, and an impressively contemporary chassis, suspension, and driveline. While the rest of the automotive world was rushing as quickly into the future as possible, Mercedes-Benz had paused just long enough to give prewar classic elegance one last hurrah.

The 300 Sc, which was introduced late in 1955 as a 1956 model, brought about sweeping changes, proof that Daimler-Benz was continually improving its cars, even if it was only going to build 200 of them! The 3.0-liter, six-cylinder overhead cam engine was now fuel-injected and displayed the boldly lettered *Einspritzmotor* emblem across the rear bumper. The new engine was closely related to that of the 300 SL, utilizing a Bosch injection pump in place of the three Solex 40 PBIC down-draft carburetors used in the 300 S. With a compression ratio increased from 7.8:1 to 8.55:1, the Sc developed 175 horsepower at 5,400 rpm, bettering the S by 25

horsepower from the same 182.7-ci displacement. Power was delivered through a fully synchronized four-speed manual transmission, with either a standard column or sportier floor-mounted shift available. Rear axle ratios changed with the introduction of the Sc to a lower 4.44:1 from the previous 4.125:1, and the addition of fuel injection also increased torque from 170 to 188 ft-lb. Mercedes-Benz literature for the 1956 models later claimed 200 horsepower for the Sc engine and a top speed of 112 miles per hour. Despite a curb weight of up to 4,450 pounds, a 300 Sc could deliver its occupants from 0 to 60 miles per hour in a respectable 14 seconds.

Comfort and performance were also given greater consideration in the Sc, which introduced a new and more responsive independent rear suspension design, utilizing a single low-pivot point rear swing axle with coil springs. The single-pivot IRS was adapted the following year for the new 300 SL Roadster. As an added convenience on Sc models, a driver-controlled electric motor connected to supplementary torsion bars adjusted the posture of the rear suspension to compensate for the added weight of passengers or luggage.

Aside from the engine changes and the use of larger brake drums to scrub off speed, the 300 S and Sc shared the same specifications of design and were available in similar models: Cabriolet, Coupe, and Roadster. Both models had a wheelbase of 114.2 inches, an overall length of 185 inches, and a front and rear track measuring 58.2 and 60.0 inches, respectively.

From September 1958 the 300 SL Roadster was offered with a removable hardtop and when so equipped was cataloged as a 300 SL Coupé. DaimlerChrysler Classic

89

Say what you will about the wickedness and temperament of old Italian sports cars; no matter how troublesome they are mechanically, the strength of their styling has always brought us devoutly to our knees in admiration.

The Italian carrozziera have always been on the cutting edge of automotive styling, but never was it more apparent than after World War II, when Vignale, Touring, Pinin Farina, Scaglietti, Ghia, and Bertone gave the world the most magnificent sports cars ever designed.

One of Italy's most respected houses was Pinin Farina, descended from the original Stabilimenti Farina, which had opened its doors in 1930. Battista Farina was the youngest of the Farina brothers and later established his own carrozzeria, which became the principal design house for Ferrari. "Pinin," the affectionate diminutive for the smallest of the brothers, was founder Giovanni Battista Farina's nickname, one that became so well recognized that by the early 1950s it had been consolidated into one word, and in 1961, both the family and company name were legally changed to Pininfarina.

From its humble beginnings, the firm specialized in the design and construction of one-off prototypes and limited editions. In less than a decade, the Farina name became one of the most respected in Italy. By 1939 the factory, with more than 500 employees, was producing one car per day.

In the early postwar years, Pinin Farina was responsible for the first and perhaps most significant new design of the era, the 1947 Cisitalia, which became the cornerstone of sports car styling for nearly a decade.

Although the designing and building of coachwork for principals like Alfa Romeo, Fiat, Lancia, and Ferrari kept prosperity at Pinin Farina's door, the attraction to foreign markets after the war was irresistible. By the early 1950s, Battista Farina had become the first Italian to design an American automobile, the Nash Ambassador. This was followed by the magnificent Nash-Healey sports car, which combined an American-made driveline with Italian coachwork and a chassis designed and built in England by Donald Healey.

It was, however, show cars like the Cisitalia that continued to bring the world to Pinin Farina's doorstep. In 1955 the carrozzeria produced another benchmark in contemporary design, this time by rebodying a 1955 Mercedes-Benz 300b. The styling of the Pininfarina Coupé was more advanced than anything Mercedes-Benz had built up to that time, with the exception of the 300 SL.

The 300 series was the most luxurious model line Mercedes-Benz had to offer, with flowing fenders and dignified Sindelfingen coachwork still influenced by prewar styling traditions. The 1955 Pininfarina-bodied 300b, and 300 Sc, produced in 1956, were a generation ahead in body design.

The styling of the Pinin Farina Coupé has been interpreted as an composite of many different cars from the period, in particular the Bentley Continental in profile, Facel Vega from the rear, and overall very reminiscent of the Alfa Romeo 6C 2500 Sport and Super Sport models bodied by Pinin Farina in the late 1940s.

Sergio Pininfarina, who succeeded his father as head of the international design firm in 1966, says that Pininfarina became very famous because its prototypes were exhibited at all the important motor shows throughout Europe. "This brought us private commissions to duplicate the prototype designs. My father believed that a car produced in a certain quantity was better than a one-off example." Sergio Pininfarina says, however, that the production of prototypes was his father's greatest ambition. "In the 1950s we began to work with all the automobile manufacturers, not only in Italy, but in Europe with Peugeot, in England with British Leyland, and with Nash in the United States. The success of that car in America had a great effect in Italy, because here a success in a foreign country is highly regarded. And we had these types of successes with many foreign automakers. We estimate that there are more than 25 million automobiles today with the Pininfarina name." The number of Pininfarina-bodied Mercedes is significantly less. Only three were designed and built in 1955 and 1956, each with a distinctively different body.

The 300b model was actually redone four times, as documented by photographs before it was privately sold in 1956. In stage one, as originally shown, there was virtually no chrome trim, except in the mandatory places like radiator shell, bumpers, wheel and window trim. Even the headlamp bezels were painted. In stage two, the headlamp bezels were all chrome, and that was the only noted change. The third stage saw the addition of

well-placed lower side molding, flat chrome bands wrapping around the front of the fenders, and extended chrome fairings on the auxiliary lamps. The fourth stage was as it appeared in the European motor shows and as it appears today, with wheel well moldings and another belt molding to facilitate two-toning of the hood and deck.

As to the actual construction of the car, records indicate that it was not until Sindelfingen received and approved the Pinin Farina drawings that an automobile was delivered. Whether a complete car or just a running chassis was sent to Pinin Farina is not clear. During an extensive restoration in 1990, a body identification tag was discovered under the left front kick panel. The tag number was 186.010 4500005, which indicated a 300b chassis with a sedan body built in 1954. Daimler-Benz AG records show that the automobile was sold to F.A. Saporiti, the Mercedes-Benz dealer in Milan, Italy, January 17, 1955, and shipped by rail to Turin. Saporiti then delivered the Mercedes to Pinin Farina, where a new

body was constructed. In the November 1955 issue of *Road & Track*, a photograph of this car appears on page 34, in an article titled "New . . . From Italy."

The distinctive styling of the Pininfarina Coupé is best viewed in profile, where the sleek fenderline draws your eye back to the modest kick-up forward of the C-pillar and the triple chrome moldings that accent the greenhouse. Some minor features include small trafficator lamps at the base of the C-pillars and wipers for the rear window.

Although the Pininfarina Coupé was displayed more than a year before the Mercedes-Benz 220 S was introduced, it is unlikely that the Italian car had any influence on Mercedes design. Knowing that the comparably styled Italian Coupé had come from the pen of no one less than Battista "Pinin" Farina, however, no doubt reassured Daimler-Benz that their decision to abandon traditional styling was right. By 1958 the luxurious 220 S had become the flagship of the Mercedes fleet, a ship navigating waters already charted by Pininfarina.

For the 1950s, the 300 Sc offered features precious few automakers even had on their drawing boards: four-wheel fully independent suspension, ventilated bimetal vacuum-assisted brakes, backup lights, turn signals, nonglare mirrors, and windshield washers. Inside, there were reclining seats, a signal-seeking radio, and appointments that today are rarely seen even on the most expensive automobiles.

Virtually hand-built to order, the S and Sc were far more expensive than any other Mercedes-Benz 300 models, the Sc demanding over $12,500, nearly twice that of the first 300 SL models, (which were priced at $7,000), and more than almost any other automobile sold in America. Among the rarest of Stuttgart's early postwar cars, only 760 were built between 1952 and 1958. Of the limited production 300 Sc models produced from September 1955 to April 1958, there were 98 Coupes, 53 Roadsters and just 49 Cabriolets. Perhaps one day, organizations like the Classic Car Club of America will acknowledge this, and change the final year of qualification from 1948 to 1958, allowing the 300 S and Sc to be added among the list of recognized classics.

The 300 S and Sc might have been the Mercedes flagship, but at the front line there was the lower-priced, but no less distinguished 220 S and 220 SE. The 220 S ("S" for Super) came along in May 1956,

The front runner in affordable style was the 220 S and SE series Cabriolet, the latter version offering a fuel-injected six-cylinder engine. The SE produced 130 horsepower, increased torque by 5 percent over the S, and fuel efficiency by 8 percent. As for styling, either was a striking automobile. Both versions were highly successful in the 1950s and are highly desirable collector cars today. *DaimlerChrysler Classic*

Interior appointments were done in the same fashion as in prewar Mercedes-Benz cars, with plush, roll-and-pleat leather upholstery and fine wood veneers in a choice of burlwood or straight-grain walnut lacquered to a glass-like finish. And there was never a problem fitting your suitcases into the car's steeply angled trunk. Every 300 S and Sc came with its own custom leather luggage set designed to stack in the trunk.

At the upper end of the Daimler-Benz line was the 300 Limousine, a car often chosen by foreign embassies and heads of state. The long-wheelbase Sedans were powered by a 180-horsepower version of the inline six. Production continued from 1951 to 1962. *DaimlerChrysler Classic*

Faced with the seemingly impossible task of returning Mercedes-Benz to racing prominence in the early postwar years, Rudolf Uhlenhaut created the 300 SL in one year, a car that virtually dominated European sports car racing throughout 1952. *DaimlerChrysler Classic*

Mercedes-Benz had built its reputation on magnificent, limited production automobiles in the 1920s and 1930s, but it was the smallest and least expensive model, the 170V, upon which the company would rebuild its fortunes in the postwar era. Pictured is a 1952 170 D Sedan, one of thousands produced in the early 1950s. Although not particularly fast, the 170 Diesel's torque curve was very steady, applying power over a wide range of engine speeds, with a maximum of 62 miles per hour in top gear.

the third of three new models making their debut. Along with the new 190 and 219, the 220 S, the most powerful and expensive of the trio, represented DBAG's new contemporary look, and bid farewell to the vestigial fender lines of the classic 1930s and 1940s. The new styling was integrated, with fenders and body sides forming one plane, seasoned perhaps with just a hint of classic lineage in the rear quarter panel treatment.

The new 220 S four-door Sedans, compared to most other prewar and mid-1950s cars, were quite subdued in appearance. Similar to the lower-priced 190 and 219 models, they formed the center of a model line topped by the 300 SL and the last of the luxurious 300 Sc series. For the first time in nearly two decades, Daimler-Benz had a full range of models.

The 220 S had forsaken the old concept of a separate body and frame, instead using the body as an integral part of the chassis, popularly known today as unibody construction. Although this saved weight and allowed more freedom in styling and suspension

design, the front suspension and engine were still mounted on a removable subframe.

The new 220 S Sedan was a practical design and sold well, but Mercedes stylists knew that it could also be transformed into a coupe and convertible that would attract the buyer who wanted something a bit more exclusive.

All three 220 S body styles—Sedan, Coupe, and Convertible—rode on the proven independent front and single-pivot swing axle rear suspension platform, with a coil spring at each wheel. The Sedan's 111-inch wheelbase was cut to 106.3 inches for the new Coupe and Convertible models, which measured 183.9 inches in overall length to the four-door's 187-inch stretch.

The M180 2,195-cc (133.9-ci) single-overhead cam six-cylinder engine was used in the same basic form in the Type 219, but in the 220 S, dual Solex carburetors allowed it to develop 100 horsepower, 15 more than the lower-priced model, which had a single carburetor. Bore and stroke were 3.15x2.86 inches, and

94

compression ratio 7.6:1. After August 1957 this was boosted to 8.7:1, which increased peak power to 106 for the 220 S and 90 for the 219. Maximum speed for the 220 S was 100 miles per hour.

In addition to the column-shifted four-speed manual transmission, an optional semiautomatic Hydrak clutch was available beginning in September 1957. This was one of the few weak designs to come from Daimler-Benz in the 1950s. Built by Fichtel and Sachs, the Hydrak system featured electrical control of vacuum-operated clutch engagement and disengagement—a kind of semiautomatic transmission. When the driver touched the shift lever, the clutch automatically released and the gear was shifted in the normal fashion, and when the gear lever was released the clutch reengaged. A fluid coupling allowed stopping and idling, etc., without disengaging the clutch. An interesting but somewhat complicated alternative to a fully automatic transmission, it was not very popular and proved somewhat delicate. In addition, if the

shifter was inadvertently bumped the car jumped out of gear. Over time, Mercedes dealers converted the majority of Hydrak-equipped models to traditional pedal-operated clutches, in order to appease frustrated owners who found the transmission more trouble than it was worth. Original cars are relatively rare today.

In September 1958, two years into 220 S production, the fuel-injected 220 SE version was introduced. The most advanced of the round-body models, the 220 SE was virtually identical to the 220 S, but equipped with intermittent mechanical fuel injection and a different camshaft. The Bosch two-plunger fuel injection pump rode on the left side of the engine and was driven from the cam chain. A large cast-alloy air plenum and intake pipes fed air to the intake ports. High-pressure fuel was infused, using manifold injection, rather than port injection, through a calibrated jet placed upstream of the junction of the manifold and cylinder head. The SE produced 130 horsepower, increased torque by 5 percent over the S, and fuel efficiency by 8 percent.

New postwar styling was reflected in lower-priced models like the 1955 Type 180 Limousine, a luxurious term for an otherwise typical four-door Sedan, powered by a four-cylinder 52-horsepower engine. These were not luxury cars by any means, but sensibly styled and reasonably priced models intended for mass marketing. *DaimlerChrysler Classic*

A 1955 300c Sedan sold for 23,500 marks, approximately $7,000. The option list included possibly the largest sunroof ever built. The manually operated Webasto fabric top moved along narrow tracks, folding over itself ever so neatly on the way back, to expose the entire front and rear passenger compartments. Similar sunroof designs date back to the 1920s and 1930s, both in Europe and America. Mercedes-Benz offered it as well on the 170 Sb, but few cars have used a folding sunroof on as grand a scale as the 300c. *Carl Minneci collection*

In addition to the car's regal styling, the 300c was often chosen for use by foreign embassies because of the long wheelbase and large, comfortable interior.

With the introduction of the new 220 Sb "Fin-back" Sedans, Mercedes discontinued the round-body 220 SE Sedans, but the sportier and more luxurious 220 SE Coupe and Convertible remained in production, overlapping that of the new 220 SEb through November 1960. Production of the new 220 SEb Coupes began in February 1961, and 220 SEb Convertible production commenced seven months later.

The first full decade of the postwar era had seen Mercedes-Benz return to prominence in the design and manufacture of luxury cars, diesel cars, and trucks, and the production of sports and racing cars, a feat hardly anyone but Mercedes-Benz would have thought possible in so short a time. This latter accomplishment alone was proof beyond doubt that the Silver Star was back. With one car, all that the Mercedes name had come to stand for in the late 1930s was reclaimed. It was perhaps the most remarkable automobile ever built by Daimler-Benz. It was the 300 SL.

It was the only logical solution.

Mercedes-Benz Chief Engineer Rudolf Uhlenhaut, Technical Director Fritz Nallinger, and stylist Karl Wilfert had reached an impasse. They had created the most aerodynamic sports car in the company's history, with only one minor flaw . . . there was no way for the driver and codriver to get into it!

The 220 S was introduced in 1956, the third of three new models making their public debut. The 220 series represented the new contemporary look of Mercedes-Benz. Two years into 220 S production, the fuel-injected 220 SE was added. Production continued through August 1959. Pictured is a 1959 model from the Dave Stitzer collection.

PREVIOUS PAGE:
The 300 Sc (pictured on the right) appeared late in 1955 as a 1956 model. Equipped with the fuel-injected 3.0-liter six-cylinder overhead cam engine, the Sc delivered 175 horsepower at 5,400 rpm, bettering the S by 25 horsepower from the same 182.7-ci displacement. The lower-priced companion 220 SE (left) was among the first of Mercedes' contemporarily styled models and was equipped with a fuel-injected 2.2-liter six delivering 115 horsepower. The 300 Sc was the last classically inspired design to come from the Sindelfingen werke. The design of the new 220 S and SE clearly departed from all past styling cues traditional to Daimler-Benz, save for the upright grille and three-pointed star hood ornament. *Jerry J. Moore collection*

The *Sehr Leicht*, which roughly translates as "light-weight," was built around a multitube spaceframe, which, though weighing a meager 181 pounds, was sufficiently stout to support the engine, transmission, and rear axle. Its design also created a high, wide sill that surrounded the passenger compartment, a necessary structural element that ruled out the use of conventionally hinged doors. The solution, as Wilfert later remarked, was to allow form to follow function. Entry would literally be "through the roof," using large panels hinged at the top that could be lifted straight up, allowing driver and codriver to step into the car and over the sill. The raised doors would later be described by the automotive press as looking like the wings of a gull.

It seems that behind every great sports car built during in the latter half of the twentieth century there was a guiding hand—a designer, an engineer, or someone with a dream, men like Enzo Ferrari, Sydney Allard, Sir William Lyons and his magnificent XK-120 and E-Type Jaguars, Colin Chapman and the Lotus, David Brown and the postwar Aston Martins, and, lest we forget, the cars created by that hard-driving and harder-talking Texan named Carroll Shelby.

At Daimler-Benz, men with vision had always been the company's greatest asset, and sometimes its greatest liability. But in Alfred Neubauer, Fritz Nallinger, Karl Wilfert, and Rudolf Uhlenhaut, Mercedes had an indomitable team who would bring the company into the postwar era and restore the honor of the Silver Arrows.

The son of a German bank director and an English mother, Rudolf Uhlenhaut was born July 15, 1906. Educated in Great Britain and Germany, he earned a

Daimler-Benz had pioneered the diesel automobile in the 1930s, and in the postwar era diesels continued to play a significant role in the Mercedes model line. Pictured is an 180 D, which was introduced in 1959.
DaimlerChrysler Classic

degree in mechanical engineering in 1931 from the Munich Technical Institute and began his 41-year career with Daimler-Benz that same year, as a passenger car test engineer.

His easy-going manner and reputation for finding creative solutions to engineering problems helped him to advance within five years to the position of Technical Director in charge of race car construction and testing. At the time of his appointment in 1936, Daimler-Benz race cars were being trounced so badly that the company had actually withdrawn from several events toward the end of the season. Just 30 years old when he was given the assignment of turning this situation around, Uhlenhaut accomplished his task in less than a year! By 1937 he had returned Mercedes-Benz to the competition forefront with the W 125 Grand Prix car.

In 1937 the W 125s won the Tripoli, German, Monaco, Swiss, Italian, and Masaryk Grands Prix. Uhlenhaut and his team later guaranteed Daimler-Benz dominance of Grand Prix racing for the rest of the decade, with the W154 and W163 GP cars.

It was during this period in his career that Uhlenhaut developed his driving skills to the extent that he could easily have become a champion race driver himself. By 1939 he was as fast as anyone on the Mercedes-Benz team, if not faster, and often would investigate complaints about a race car being down on speed by taking it out himself and carefully analyzing its performance from behind the wheel.

It has been written that he had been soundly admonished by his superiors, not just for test-driving race

cars, but for doing so at speeds that rivaled the factory's top drivers. By the 1950s he was in a class with World Driving Champion Juan Manuel Fangio. Of course, Uhlenhaut was far too valuable to Daimler-Benz as an engineer and designer to be put at risk in competition, which makes one wonder exactly what they thought about their drivers back then! Nevertheless, Uhlenhaut's abilities behind the wheel allowed him to develop cars not only from an engineer's perspective but that of a race driver's as well—a talent with which few designers have ever been blessed.

Phil Hill, America's first World Driving Champion, knew Uhlenhaut throughout much of his racing career in the 1950s and 1960s. Says Hill, "He was held in the highest esteem by drivers, because he was an engineer who could drive. All those stories you and I read about Uhlenhaut being able to drive Mercedes GP cars at competitive speeds around circuits such as the Nurburgring were true, and that's no mean feat."

Upon returning to work for Daimler-Benz after World War II, Rudolf Uhlenhaut was appointed chief of the experimental department. As head of research and development, he was also responsible for the factory's postwar racing program. In 1951 his prewar colleague, the legendary Alfred Neubauer, resumed direction of the works race team.

Uhlenhaut was facing a difficult challenge in his new position, that of repeating what he had done for Daimler-Benz in the 1930s with the W 125. This time, however, he had little more than production car engines and spare parts at his disposal, and a budget well below Neubauer's vision of a factory racing effort.

Even as late as 1951, Mercedes-Benz was working with fundamentally prewar designs, and its 300 series flagship models were in many respects the last vestiges of a bygone era. The first truly modern Mercedes-Benz models would not appear until 1954, thus the 1952 300 SL race cars and the production versions that followed are distinguished above all for their advanced exterior styling. It is also worth mentioning that the 190 SL Roadster appeared at the same time as the 300 SL Coupe in 1954, and this more affordable open version, sharing a similar body design, was on the market two years before the 300 SL appeared in roadster form.

Having watched Jaguar dominate the French 24-hour day-into-night marathon at Le Mans in 1951, Uhlenhaut, with his boss and close associate, Daimler-Benz Technical Director Fritz Nallinger, reasoned that

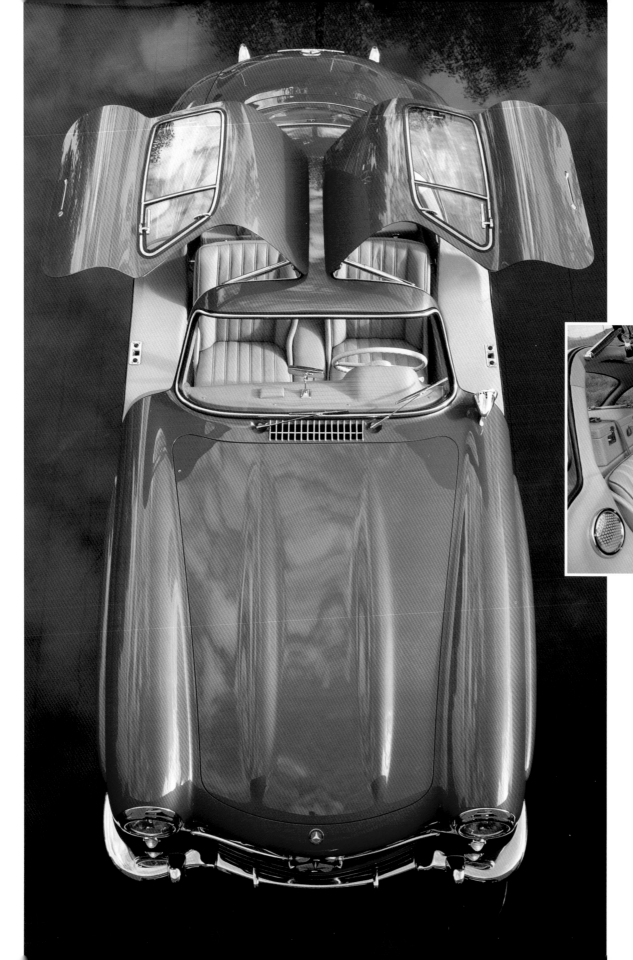

The rarest of the 300 SLs, aside from the 29 alloy Competition Coupes, were 13 cars painted strawberry red. Pictured is the finest example of this model known to exist, restored by Jerry Hjeltness Restorations in Escondido, California. The overhead view also affords one the opportunity to see the aerodynamic lines of the Karl Wilfert, Paul Braiq–designed body.

Interior upholstery choices were either gabardine plaid with tex-leather (vinyl) or hand-sewn leather throughout. The leather option was less popular in 1954 and 1955. The majority of early cars came standard with fabric seats. Two-piece leather luggage was an option that many 300 SL owners purchased. With little or no room in the trunk, the specially designed suitcases fit perfectly on the shelf behind the seats.

This is literally the very last 300 SL ever built. It was completed in 1996 from factory parts that were never assembled! The car sat, in pieces, from the time all of the components were shipped to original owner, Bob Doehler, a senior stylist at Studebaker-Packard, until being assembled by noted restorer Scott Grundfor in 1996. Studebaker-Packard became the U.S. importer for Mercedes-Benz in the mid-1950s, and Doehler decided he wanted his car shipped unassembled! If not for his position within the company, such a request would never have been granted. When Studebaker-Packard went out of business, Doehler put the car, still unassembled, in storage where it would remain, intact, until 1994 when he passed away. The new owner hired Grundfor to assemble the brand-new 1954 300 SL. Sometimes fact is stranger than fiction!

they could do essentially the same with Mercedes-Benz 300s that William Lyons had done with the XK-120 Jaguars. Raid the parts bin! The XK120C had been little more than an aerodynamic body covering a slightly modified suspension, lighter frame, and moderately tuned version of an off-the-shelf engine. In Jaguar's case it had been the double overhead cam XK-series six; for Daimler-Benz it would be the single overhead cam six from the Type 300 and 300 S. Uhlenhaut and Nallinger reasoned that the cars could also utilize other 300 S components deemed suitable for competition— rear axle, transmission, front and rear suspension, even the wheels and tires.

As a starting point, the 300 Sedan, compared to an XK-120 Jaguar, was admittedly a big, cumbersome

car, but it had the engine Mercedes needed, a 2,996-cc inline six with a compression ratio of 6.4:1 and an output of 115 horsepower at 4,600 rpm. Rugged and simple, the engine was built for sturdiness and long life. Reliability was the name of the game in endurance racing, and if nothing else, the 3-liter six was that. Although it would receive extensive modification, the final version used in the 300 SL closely relied on the original passenger car design.

Alfred Neubauer objected strongly to use of this engine. He wanted more horsepower and less weight. He also objected to the standard transmission of the 300, complained about the quality of the brakes, and criticized the diameter of the tires. All of his arguments were just, and as the 300 SL developed, Uhlenhaut and

The 300 SL had been accepted by the FIA for international competition in the Grand Turismo Class. The presence of 300 SLs at motorsport events across the United States and throughout Europe in 1955 and 1956 focused as much attention on Mercedes as had the factory's racing efforts in 1952. A total of 29 alloy-bodied cars were built for competition, like this example from Ralph Lauren's collection. The 300 SLs were entered in almost every major sports car race, scoring victories in the Mille Miglia, Liège-Rome-Liège, Alpine, and Tulip rallies in 1955. In 1956, Prince Metternich finished sixth in the rain-soaked Mille Miglia, the team of Shock and Moll won the Acropolis and Sestrière rallies, Stirling Moss finished second in the Tour de France, and Willy Mairesse won the '56 Liège-Rome-Liège contest.

Nallinger would address each of them, as Neubauer played devil's advocate to their every move.

In the end, Uhlenhaut extracted 170 horsepower from the 300 series engine without increasing its displacement, but the 300 SL's success would rely as much on engineering as sheer horsepower. In addition to a revised engine, the race car would require a lightweight frame and a streamlined body to become a winner. Uhlenhaut and Nallinger already had the weight problem solved with the birdcage-like spaceframe, and chief stylist Karl Wilfert was applying his experience in aerodynamics to a sleek, streamlined body design. All that remained was to fit the pieces together like some elaborate jigsaw puzzle.

In building the 300 SL, numerous parts and components were taken directly from the 300 Sedan's parts bin. For the front axle, the only modifications required were holes drilled in the upper spring and shock supports for weight reduction. The gearbox and long-arm shifter were taken from the Sedan without significant modification.

Interior of the alloy cars was identical to standard steel and aluminum-bodied Gullwings, with the exception of racing harnesses and when fitted, dash-mounted timing clocks.

The 300 SL Gullwing Coupe was a brilliant idea—the 300 SL Roadster was inspired! The new model, which replaced the Coupe in 1957, was an improved design with better handling and more comfort and convenience.

The revised 300 SL design featured a new rear suspension, which improved ride and handling characteristics. The spaceframe was also slightly modified to accommodate the new roadster body. Prominently featured in Mercedes-Benz advertising, between 1957 and 1964, a total of 1,858 were built. *DaimlerChrysler Classic*

Another unchanged feature was the cast-iron gearbox. Uhlenhaut simply added an oil pump and modified the gear profiles to cope with the higher torque.

One area where the Sedan's design had little influence was the 300 SL's track. Uhlenhaut had this to consider: While a narrow track would help reduce frontal area, the rear axle required a wide track to counter the significant weakness of the swing axle and the car's propensity (when cornered smartly) to swap ends. Uhlenhaut and his drivers knew that a wider rear track was the only way to reduce the swing axle's significant—and undesirable—changes of rear wheel camber. The final result was a compromise: front track was 1,340 millimeters (52.76 inches), and rear track was 1,445 millimeters (56.89 inches). The first few cars built were fitted with five stud disc wheels, which were replaced as soon as possible by light alloy rims using a central locking hub (knock-off) with 6.70x15 tires. The choice of tire dimensions had also been a concession. While Neubauer had insisted on 16-inch tires, offering the advantage of lower operating temperatures, the final decision was to stick with the 15-inch tires from the Sedan. This offered twin advantages of lower unsprung weight and a tiny reduction of the swing axle's nasty habits.

The next hurdle was the engine. The inline six was too tall for the car. Uhlenhaut's solution to that problem was to tilt the engine 40 degrees to the left,[1] moving the crankshaft to the right of the car's centerline, thus killing the proverbial two birds with one stone. The car became lower and its center of mass was now almost exactly in the center! Another advantage was that this gave the driver more legroom, albeit at the passenger's expense. The final result ensured that the six-cylinder engine could devote more horsepower to speed and less to overcoming the car's aerodynamic drag.

The sleek, rounded contours of the body were a perfect match for Uhlenhaut's tubular spaceframe. Slipping through the air, the 300 SL carried no superfluous cargo, no chrome-plated bumpers, door handles, outside rear-view mirrors—nothing that might increase resistance. The wind tunnel revealed a drag coefficient of 0.25, a figure that auto manufacturers still find challenging today!

Mercedes-Benz campaigned the 300 SLs for only one season, in which they finished first and second in all but their maiden race, the grueling Mille Miglia, where they finished second—just four minutes behind Giovani Bracco's winning Ferrari. From then on, the Mercedes-Benz team never saw the exhaust of another car across the finish line. They finished 1-2-3 at the Grand Prix of Berne, and 1-2 at Le Mans. At the Nürburgring, the team crossed the finish line in order, first through fourth. Having proven themselves virtually unbeatable in Europe, the Mercedes team concluded the 1952 season on the other side of the Atlantic competing in the Carrera PanAmericana. The 300 SL was untried in the desert, and the race was fraught with bizarre problems from the start. (On the first leg, from Tuxtla Gutiérrez to Oaxaca, a buzzard crashed through the windshield of Karl Kling's 300 SL and landed in his codriver's lap.) The Mercedes-Benz team, nevertheless, managed a remarkable 1-2 finish, moving through the desert so fast that racing manager Alfred Neubauer's chartered DC 3 spotter plane could barely keep up.

From the very beginning the subject of producing the 300 SL as a road car had been considered. With a little added persuasion from U.S. importer Max Hoffman, the board gave Uhlenhaut and his design staff the go-ahead to turn the championship race car into a sports car.

For Mercedes-Benz, the New York world debut of the production version 300 SL on February 6, 1954, at the International Motor Sports Show, was an unprecedented break with tradition. This was the first time the company had ever introduced a new model in the United States before showing it in Germany! And while New York in the throes of winter might have seemed an unlikely venue, this was the home of Max Hoffman, the man who almost single-handedly established the German automotive market in the United States.

With an elegant Frank Lloyd Wright-designed showroom situated in the heart of New York City, Austro-American importer and automotive entrepreneur Max Hoffman had been responsible for bringing Porsche, Jaguar, and Alfa Romeo to the United States in the early 1950s. Having seen the 300 SLs race in 1952, he was convinced that a road-going version would sell in the United States as quickly as Mercedes could build them. And he was correct. Of the 1,400 Coupes produced through 1957, Hoffman sold roughly 1,000.

The change from race car to road car demanded numerous revisions to the engine and fragile lightweight body, yet the fraternal relationship between the 300 SLs that had swept the 1952 racing calendar and those that would dazzle sports car cognoscenti was unmistakable. The production 300 SL, itself a worthy competitor, was accepted by the FIA for international competition in the Grand Turismo Class. With cars in the hands of privateer racers, Mercedes-Benz SLs continued to dominate motorsports throughout the early 1950s, as sports car racing became an American passion.

With a maximum of 215-horsepower from the 300 SL's direct fuel-injected six-cylinder engine, the cars could easily top 150 miles per hour, making them the fastest production sports cars available at the time.

Stylists Karl Wilfert and Paul Braiq had done a remarkable job of turning a purpose-built race car into a civilized, road-going sports car, but underneath the streamlined bodywork and luxuriously appointed interior, the 300 SL was very much unchanged. Driver and passenger still had to clamber over the wide elbow-high door sill—always a test of one's patience and grace—baggage was restricted to what could be packed behind the seats or folded into the optional leather luggage, and in general, unless one had the skills of Stirling Moss, driving the 300 SL properly and effectively was no easy task.

The 300 SL Roadster was a long time coming, but there was little doubt that a demand existed. This had been proven since 1954, when the 190 SL Roadster made its debut. Produced into the early 1960s, Mercedes-Benz delivered more than 25,000 of the sporty four-cylinder Convertibles. *DaimlerChrysler Classic*

and headroom being the biggest—while an improved rear suspension for the Roadsters made the 300 SL more manageable. The Coupe had used a conventional swing-axle with two pivot points outboard of the differential. If driven on trailing throttle through a tight curve, the camber change tended to lift the inside rear wheel and induce sudden oversteer, the same problem the race drivers had encountered. This was manageable for professionals, but detrimental to those less skilled, so the Roadster was fitted with a new swing axle, utilizing a single low pivot point, thereby improving the car's cornering behavior and predictability. A horizontal compensating spring included with the new axle also gave the Roadster a somewhat gentler ride. Improvements in the engine compartment, including a standard-equipment sports camshaft, provided an additional 20 horsepower, making it not only a better-handling car than its predecessor, but a quicker one too, despite a 200-pound weight penalty. Although not as competitive as the Gullwing, the Roadster was the more comfortable and practical of the two 300 SL models. With the addition of Dunlop disc brakes in March 1961, and an optional removable hardtop, the Roadster reached its highest level of development—the final evolution of the cars that had come from the parts bin, and the imagination of Uhlenhaut, Nallinger, and Wilfert. Produced through 1962, a total of 1,858 300 SL Roadsters were built.

Daimler-Benz had set its sights on the American market around the same time the 300 SL was introduced in New York, with the intent of establishing its own marketing network. This would eliminate Hoffman, who also represented BMW, Jaguar, Porsche, and Alfa Romeo, from the equation. This began in the fall of 1954 when Heinz Hoppe was sent to the United States to lay the groundwork. It began with an alliance between Daimler-Benz and a struggling American automaker in need of something to boost its flagging image—Studebaker-Packard. The agreement drawn up between the two companies in 1957 instantly gave Mercedes-Benz a distribution network of 2,500 dealers. Unfortunately, Studebaker-Packard salesmen hadn't a clue how to sell foreign cars, or to handle the temperamental nature of customers interested in such unusual automobiles. The "marriage made in heaven" was slowly heading toward the nether regions, but Hoppe managed to keep it working for nearly a

Toward the end of 300 SL production, Hoffman queried Mercedes-Benz regarding a roadster model similar to the 190 SL, which would be better suited to the needs of American drivers. Unknown to Hoffman, or anyone outside Rudolf Uhlenhaut's design studio, a roadster version of the 300 SL had actually been on the drawing boards since 1954. Thus in 1957 the Gullwing was replaced by the new 300 SL Roadster. As Hoffman had anticipated, it was a larger version of the four-cylinder-powered 190 SL Roadster that had been introduced in 1955. And it, too, was a success in America.

As a convertible, most of the problems associated with the Gullwing were remedied—ventilation

The 220 S and SE sedans, like the 1959 220 SE pictured, were quite subdued in appearance compared to other Mercedes-Benz models of the 1950s, similar in styling to the lower-priced 180 D through 219 models. Together they formed the center of a model line topped by the 300 SL and the last of the luxurious 300 Sc series. With the introduction of the new 220 Sb "Finback" sedans, Mercedes discontinued the round-body 220 SE sedans. *Frank Barrett Collection.*

decade, establishing Mercedes-Benz Sales Inc. in 1958 as a subsidiary of Studebaker-Packard. When the South Bend automaker folded its tents in 1964 and moved what remained of its operations to Canada, Hoppe convinced the Daimler-Benz board to act quickly and separate itself from the ill-fated company (through a $3.75 million buyout of the contract still binding Mercedes to Studebaker-Packard). This done, in April 1965, Hoppe and his staff established Mercedes-Benz of North America as a separate company. They selected the best of the former Studebaker-Packard dealers to be the first Mercedes-Benz dealerships in the United States.

In the years from 1946 to 1960, Mercedes-Benz had managed to rebuild itself and its self-image, not only in Europe but in America. The company's success throughout its first full postwar decade, on both road and track, would set the course for the future and a new era in Daimler-Benz history.

The 1950s came to an end with the introduction of a new generation of Mercedes styling, known as the finback. This was the first gesture toward the American influence of the era and a bold departure from the previous designs coming from the Daimler-Benz design center in Sindelfingen. *DaimlerChrysler Classic*

CHAPTER SEVEN

The 1960s

Redefining Sports and Elegance

Compared to the 1960s we aren't living—
we're just getting through each day.
—Anonymous

ore happened in any one year during the 1960s than in the entire decade of the 1950s combined. And that's not an exaggeration, not if one considers the sweeping sociopolitical revolution that came about during that remarkable 10-year period. Music changed. Television changed. Movies changed. World governments changed. America nearly went to war over the Cuban missile crisis, and shortly thereafter had to deal with the first presidential assassination since William McKinley in 1901. Americans set foot on the Moon, but couldn't set foot in East Berlin. Ralph Nader's book, *Unsafe at Any Speed*, was published in 1965.

Although the 300 SL had been born a product of the postwar era, it was produced into the early 1960s as the 300 SL Roadster, pictured with top down, in the background, and with the later removable hardtop shown on the black car. Successor to the original Gullwing, a car that had become legendary in its own time, Mercedes-Benz now had to face the task of replacing the 300 SL in 1963. *Pat Smiekel collection*

109

Fondly referred to today as the "finback," the first new generation of Mercedes-Benz models in the 1960s featured finely decorated exterior styling, American-inspired tailfins, and a variety of engines ranging from a fuel-efficient 1.9-liter diesel to the top-of-the line 3-liter six. Although popular in Europe, the body design never quite caught on in the United States, and by 1965 a new generation of cars would bow. *DaimlerChrysler Classic*

It criticized the American auto industry for its lack of progress in the area of automotive safety, singling out the Chevrolet Corvair for his most blistering attack. The book would have several long-term effects (as it seems would Nader!), the most punishing being the demise of the Corvair and the public's faith in Detroit. Nader would also pave the way for the consumer movement of the 1960s, which continues to influence both American and European cars to this day. In 1966 the National Traffic and Motor Vehicle Safety Act and the Highway Safety Act were passed, and the Department of Transportation was established.

The 1960s became a decade of enlightenment, of misguided trust, of a war that would divide a nation. Against this backdrop the automobile was changing as well. For Mercedes, the 1960s would be a decade underscored by improvements in design and engineering that would bring to market some of the most legendary cars to come from the world's oldest automaker.

Although it was often said throughout the twentieth century, in the aftermath of one event or another, that *things would never be the same*—during the 1960s, it was true.

For Daimler and Benz, progress in the design and development of the automobile had rarely been a problem. After all, they'd invented the thing! During the first half of the twentieth century Daimler and Benz, both individually and together, had set the standards for the world with cars such as the 1901 Mercedes, the

Blitzen Benz, SSKL, 540 K, and the 300 SL. At the time, it might have appeared as though there wasn't much left to do, so Daimler-Benz started the new decade with a celebration.

In February 1961, some 35 years after the two oldest automobile companies in Germany merged to form Daimler-Benz AG, the 75th anniversary of the Benz Patent Motorwagen was celebrated with the opening of the new Daimler-Benz Automotive Museum in Stuttgart and the public introduction of a new model, the Mercedes-Benz 220 SE Coupe.

The all-new 220 SEb, also referred to as "the Jubilee Year Mercedes," differed greatly from the 220 SE Coupe it replaced in 1961. It was a handsome, prestigious version of the 220 SE Sedan, with two doors, four seats, and a sleek new body—a perfect synthesis of sports car and touring car. A fuel-injected, 134-horsepower 2.2-liter overhead cam, six-cylinder engine, and floor-mounted four-speed shifter provided sports car-like performance, in vivid contrast to the luxuriously appointed interior, finished with leather upholstery and fine burlwood trim.

Although built in the same fashion as the previous 220 models, with unitized body construction, single joint low pivot swing axle independent rear and traditional Mercedes independent front suspension, the new SEb Coupe and Cabriolet rode on a 2-1/2 inch-longer wheelbase (108-1/2 inches), and were 8 inches longer at 192-1/2 inches, some 3 inches wider, at 72.7

Elegance had a new name in 1963. It was Mercedes-Benz 600. Powered by the company's first production fuel-injected V-8, the 6.3-liter engine delivered 250 horsepower at 4,000 rpm, every bit of which was needed to carry the luxurious Sedan, Pullman, and Landaulet coachwork built at Sindelfingen. The model pictured is the 600 Sedan. *DaimlerChrysler Classic*

The longer-wheelbase Pullman was available in two versions, Limousine and Pullman-Landaulet, a custom-built parade car with a folding rear quarter-roof. *DaimlerChrysler Classic*

inches, and 3 inches lower, measuring just 56.1 inches at the roof. It was the design ideology that GM's legendary Harley Earl had preached throughout his career—"longer, lower, wider." Someone at Daimler-Benz had listened.

Mechanically, the new SEb was the first Mercedes model to offer front disc brakes. In most other respects, it was unchanged from its predecessor, powered by a 2.2-liter six with Bosch intermittent induction-manifold injection, and an output of 134 horsepower at 5,000 rpm, providing both Coupe and Cabriolet with honest sports car acceleration right up to their maximum speed of 105 miles per hour.

Bruno Sacco, who had joined the Sindelfingen design staff in 1958, recalled, "[The 1961 Coupe] was one of the most beautiful Mercedes ever designed, but not only that: It was one of the most beautiful cars ever designed anywhere. The proportions were just right, and there were no transient styling elements except for

the buffers attached to the four corners of the vehicle."

In his 1988 book, *Mercedes-Benz Design*, Sacco wrote, "The vertically arranged headlight unit, introduced with the 300 SL Roadster, reached its height with the 220 SEb. Also of particular interest was the horizontal arrangement of the very large rear light unit," a styling cue that Sacco would revisit many times during his years as director of design.

While the merits of any automotive design are purely conjectural . . . *What plays well in Stuttgart might*

When in Germany, leave the Daimler at home. When Queen Elizabeth II visited West Germany, she was provided with a luxurious 600 Pullman-Landaulet. *DaimlerChrysler Classic*

In 1963 the 300 SL and 190 SL Roadsters bowed out of the model line, replaced by a single car, the all-new, and very different, 230 SL. A striking departure from the smooth, rounded contours of the 300 SL and 190 SL, the squared-off 230 SL, with its removable "pagoda" roof, kicked off a new era of Mercedes-Benz sports car design. The motor press wasn't impressed, so Mercedes-Benz decided to put on a little demonstration . . . *DaimlerChrysler Classic*

be received less charitably in Des Moines . . . few will argue that the 220 SEb Coupe was as near perfect a blend of form and function as any automaker in the early 1960s ever achieved.

Perhaps the greatest challenge Mercedes-Benz faced in the early 1960s was creating a suitable successor to one of the greatest sports cars ever conceived. Since 1957 the archetypal German sports car had been the 300 SL Roadster. Or had it? Against total sales of 1,858 cars built over a span of six years, the 190 SL, priced exactly half that of the 300 SL, had achieved a sales level of 25,881 cars in eight years—a very disproportionate number. Thus the problem was determining which SL roadster needed to be replaced. With Solomon-like wisdom, Rudolf Uhlenhaut managed to replace both with a single car.

His plan was to combine the performance of the 300 SL with the high production capability and affordability of the sporty little 190 SL. These characteristics, together with all new styling and improved handling, brought to the highways the next generation Mercedes sports car, the 230 SL.

On its own, the 230 SL and later 250 and 280 variants were consummate examples of Mercedes-Benz design and engineering. Cars that had been well thought out, but in the eyes of many sports car cognoscenti still smitten with the 300 SL, not an altogether suitable heir. The 230 SL not only had to live up to the 300 SL's image, it had the misfortune of arriving at the same time as Jaguar's new XK-E and Chevrolet's Corvette Stingray, two sports cars of decidedly different character than the Mercedes, but arguably better suited to the image most had come to associate with high-performance two-seaters.

Mercedes-Benz had a difficult mission. To fill the shoes of a legendary automobile and bridge the gap between one that had been more race car than boulevardier with another that by its very design would be regarded as a more civilized, contemporary road car.

Introduced at the Geneva Auto Show in March 1963, the 230 SL was more than it appeared to be, but less than the motor press had expected. Where there once had been a sleek, curvaceous, race-bred roadster now stood a squared-off two-seater powered by a single overhead cam 2.3-liter six-cylinder engine developing only 150 horsepower. Despite the fact that the car had better handling, vastly improved comfort, and a higher level of options, most found the 230 SL an unlikely candidate to win the hearts of 300 SL owners.

Perhaps knowing this beforehand, Mercedes-Benz wasted little time in proving the car's mettle, entering a virtually stock 230 SL in the legendary *Spa-Sofia-Liège* Rally—Europe's equivalent of the Carrera PanAmericana for its sheer abuse to driver and machine. Just as the 300 SLs had been victorious in 1952, speeding to victory through the Mexican desert, the 230 SL, with driver Eugen Böhringer, claimed a decisive win in this most grueling of European endurance races. This left little doubt that the new car was cut from the same cloth as the great 300 SL. It was, however, sewn in a very different fashion.

The 230 SL followed a different road than its predecessor, or for that matter, any of its contemporaries. Built on a comparatively short 94.5-inch wheelbase, the 230 SL had a very wide track, 58.3 inches front and

The 220 SE, recalled retired Daimler-Benz director of design Bruno Sacco, "was one of the most beautiful Mercedes ever designed, but not only that: it was one of the most beautiful cars ever designed anywhere. The vertically arranged headlight unit, introduced with the 300 SL Roadster, reached its height with the 220 SE."
DaimlerChrysler Classic

...Mercedes-Benz took a virtually stock 230 SL and entered it in the Spa-Sofia-Liège, Europe's equivalent of the Carrera PanAmericana for its sheer abuse to driver and machine. When the dust cleared, Mercedes team driver Eugen Böhringer had claimed a decisive win, thus dismissing any doubts about the car's capabilities.
DaimlerChrysler Classic

Mercedes-Benz interior design had reached another high watermark in the 1960s with beautiful leather upholstery; burlwood trim around the dashboard, windshield, and doors; and the large steering wheel for which Mercedes would come to be known.

FAR LEFT:
The last of the models designed in the late 1950s was the first series 220 SE produced through 1960. Among the rarer examples was the 2/2 Coupe with sunroof. Mercedes manufactured 3,916 220 SE models from 1958 to 1960, consisting of 1,974 Sedans, 1,112 Cabriolets, and 830 Coupes. At the top of the line in 1960, the average price for a Mercedes-Benz 220 SE was $9,000.

58.5 inches rear. The car's stance was some 8 inches wider than that of the new E-Type Jaguar. The result was an exceptionally well-mannered two-seater with very predictable handling, a better transmission, and better brakes than the 300 SL.

As had been the practice since the early 1930s, Mercedes-Benz sports cars rode on a suspension independently mounted at all four wheels. The 230 SL used an advanced low pivot swing-axle rear suspension with semi-trailing arms, coil springs, and telescopic deCarbon shock absorbers. The front suspension consisted of wishbones, coil springs, telescopic deCarbon shock absorbers, and an antisway bar. The deCarbon shocks were later replaced with Bilstein shock absorbers on the 250 SL and 280 SL models.

As good as they were, the 230, 250, and 280 SL never achieved the status of the 300 SL. It was perhaps no great loss because the cars appealed to a greater number of people, and outsold the 300 SL Coupe and Roadster by better than 15 to 1.

Where the Gullwing had essentially been regarded as a man's car, and a man with exceptional driving skills

The 220 SE name was derived from the displacement of the engine, 2.2 liters, multiplied by 100, the "S" indicating that this car was senior to the firm's lower-priced models. "E" denoted *Einspritzung* for fuel injection. In 1961, Mercedes produced a total of 2,537 220 SEb models, (SEb is the correct nomenclature for the second generation 220 SE). The 220 SEb offered redesigned coachwork with contemporary fenderlines, a lower, sportier stance, wide pillarless side windows, and more discrete use of chrome. All that remained of the previous design was the traditional Mercedes-Benz grille. The new models were produced from September 1960 through October 1965 and totaled 14,173 coupes and 2729 convertibles.

When the 230 SL was introduced as a successor to the 300 SL, Mercedes-Benz knew there would be some resistance, so they prepared a new 230 SL and sent driver Eugen Böhringer to the grueling Spa-Sofia-Liège Rally, to demonstrate the car's performance and durability in Europe's toughest road race. It was a gamble that paid off for Mercedes. Böhringer won and the world took note. The car pictured is a duplicate of the model campaigned in 1963 and is displayed in the Mercedes-Benz Museum.

at that, the 300 SL and 190 SL Roadsters had cleared the way for an entirely different market, one that would be ideally suited to the more contemporary 230, 250 and 280 SL. They were immediately more popular with women than the 300 SL had ever been, and among those who wanted a sports car but not the sports car compromises, the new SL was just the thing. In the end there were more 230, 250, and 280 SLs seen at country clubs than at racetracks. From 1963 to 1971, Mercedes-Benz sold 48,912 of the sporty 230, 250, and 280 SL models. Even factoring in 190 SL sales, the figures were still nearly twice that of the earlier models. If success were measured in units sold, in this race the 230, 250, and 280 SL had handily defeated their predecessors.

What primarily differentiated the 230, 250, and 280 SL was power. When the marketplace demanded more from the 230 SL, Mercedes responded with increased displacement. The 2.3 became a 2.5 in 1966 and a 2.8 in 1968, explaining the 250 and 280 designations. Oddly enough, none of the later versions ever surpassed the first 230 SL in performance, even though the 280 SL had 170 horsepower. In the June 1963 issue of *Road & Track*, a 230 SL equipped with the four-speed manual transmission and 3.75:1 ratio was tested. It established a 0 to 60 time of 9.7 seconds and a top

The 300 SL had used a six-cylinder engine that produced a maximum of 240 horsepower. While the new six under the hood of the 230 SL developed only 150 horsepower, the car was an overall improvement in terms of suspension, handling, and braking. Although not as fast, what it lost in the straight it made up for in the corners.

117

speed of 124 miles per hour. When the *R&T* staff tested a 280 SL in August 1968, best 0 to 60 was 9.9 seconds and top speed was down to 114 miles per hour. What happened? It seemed that somewhere along the way the 280 SL had gained 65 kilograms, about 140 pounds, in unsprung weight, just enough to offset the additional 20 horsepower provided by the 2.8-liter engine. In the sales brochures, 170 horsepower looked better than 150, and most customers were buying the 280 SL for image, so few would ever experience the car

at its limits. Perhaps more significantly, with the passing of three decades since their introduction, the 230, 250, and 280 SLs appear neither out of date nor out of place on the road, and unlike the 300 SL and 190 SL, most are still being driven regularly.

Was it a sports car or not? If you judge by the motoring press, you can only come to one conclusion. Yes. In August 1967, *Sports Car Graphic* suggested that the car could be competitive in SCCA competition, in F Production, where the 230 SL was classified. "To return

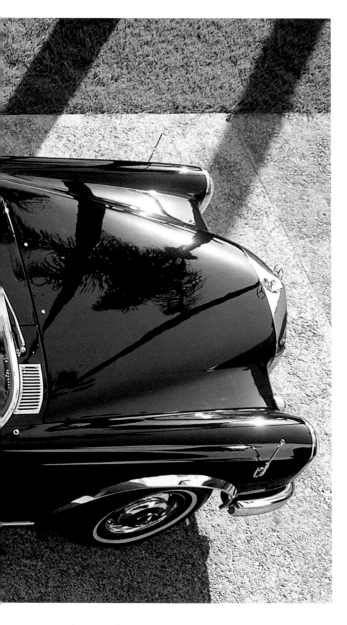

Throughout the first half of the twentieth century, Mercedes-Benz had taken on many different roles—builder of world-beating racing and sports cars; manufacturer of the finest touring cars; and the company to which heads of state and captains of industry turned for the finest automobiles, therefore it was necessary that Mercedes-Benz rekindle its old successes again and again. In 1963 it did just that with the debut of the Type 600.

Without question, the 600 was one of greatest achievements in Mercedes-Benz history. Luxury and performance were inspired by the great 770 Grosser Mercedes of the 1930s; like its acclaimed predecessor, the 600 was built for an exclusive clientele of royals, government leaders, and those of immense wealth, and then only in limited numbers. In its 18-year life span, from August 1963 to June 1981, the longest for a single Mercedes-Benz model, only 2,677 were built. Production of the 600 ran highest in 1965, when 345 Limousines and 63 Pullmans were delivered. The last 600 built, a short-wheelbase Sedan, went straight into the Mercedes-Benz Museum.

Prominent names associated with the 600 include King Hussein, Mao Tse-tung, Queen Elizabeth II, the Shah of Iran, Marshal Tito, Prince Rainier, and the president of Rumania. They were frequently used by foreign embassies as official state cars, and in 1965, the Vatican received a special 600 Pullman Landaulet for the use of Pope Paul VI. The 600 remained the official car of the Vatican for 20 years, after which it was donated to the Mercedes-Benz Museum, where it is prominently displayed today.

A mechanically fuel-injected, overhead cam V-8 having a swept volume of 6,330 cc, or 386 ci, powered

The new Model 600 was the most lavishly appointed production automobile ever manufactured by Mercedes. This unusual plan view shows the immense size of the rare six-door Pullman-Landaulet, the most elaborate of the three 600 versions produced. To put the value of these cars in perspective, the price of a Pullman Limousine in 1963 was approximately $18,000. By the time production concluded in 1981, the average price of a 600 in the United States had risen to over $100,000.

to the everyday aspects of the car," said *SCG*, "it'd be easy to sum up as 'faultless.'" *Car and Driver* wrote, "Every driver who has more than a purely utilitarian interest in automobiles should drive a Mercedes-Benz 250 SL at least once in his life. The car is an almost perfect yardstick against which to measure any other car." And *Road & Track* delivered the consummate summation of the 280 SL by writing, "For those who value engineering finesse and high-quality construction, it's alone in the field."

The driver compartment was beautifully appointed and there was an intercom with a microphone conveniently placed on the steering column, so the chauffeur could respond without removing his hands from the wheel.

119

Offering similar styling but greater performance, the 330 SE Coupe was one of the most handsome of all Mercedes-Benz models produced in the 1960s. Almost identical to the 220 SEb Coupe, the car was powered by 3.0-liter inline six similar in layout to that used in the 300 SL sports cars, including a seven-main bearing crankshaft, light alloy block, and aluminum cast head. The main difference was in the fuel delivery. The 300 SL had fuel injection directly into the cylinders, while the 300 SE used a manifold injection system.

the 600 models. The 90-degree design, designated M100, had a compression ratio of 9.0:1, bore and stroke of 103x95 millimeters, and a peak output of 300 horsepower at 4,000 rpm. Peak torque was a colossal 434 ft-lb, delivered at 3,000 rpm. More significant, perhaps, than the car itself, this was the first production V-8 engine Mercedes-Benz had ever built. It was used exclusively in the 600 series until 1968, after which it appeared in what can only be described as the first high-performance sports sedan ever built, the 300 SEL 6.3.

The suspension for the 600 utilized compressor-fed air units. Brakes were discs all around with twin calipers at each front wheel, and tires were 9.00x15 radials on 6-1/2x15 wheels. The enormous Sedans and Pullmans consumed fuel at an average of 10 miles per gallon from an oversize tank accommodating just under 30 gallons. To help provide power for the many auxiliary systems, the engine drove two alternators, one on the left, the other on the right. A total of five vee belts drove the twin alternators, the air-conditioning compressor, the hydraulic pump, the cooling fan, and the air compressor.

Daimler-Benz's director of passenger car development, Rudolf Uhlenhaut, once said that the cost of building the 600 was of secondary importance. Virtually every part used in the cars was designed and built especially for that model. According to Uhlenhaut, the 600's design demanded "sufficient room for tall people; the best possible suspension; low body roll while cornering; a wide range of adjustability for all seats; well functioning ventilation, heating and air conditioning; silent operation of the whole car, and power assistance for all manual operations."

In terms of performance, the criteria were no less demanding. The 600 would require good roadholding, precise power-assisted steering, superior braking ability, tires suited to continued high-speed driving, adequate acceleration, strong body construction, and interior safety measures. After all, some of the most important people in the world would be riding in them.

It was perhaps unlike any other car built in its time. The 600's four-wheel independent and height-adjustable suspension provided an uncompromisingly smooth ride for passengers under virtually all road conditions, thus settings for the hydraulic shock absorbers could be varied from soft to firm via a three-position lever located on the steering column. And should conditions demand extra ground clearance, the car could be raised 2 inches by the pneumatic air bag system that also kept the vehicle level no matter what the load.

Bringing the 600 to a stop was a sophisticated dual-circuit hydraulic power disc brake system consisting of separate front and rear units operated by compressed air. The parking brake was automatically released when the gear lever was moved from Neutral. A compressed air horn warned off anyone who dared delay a 600 and its occupants.

Each was equipped with an array of special features, such as central vacuum locking for doors and trunk. Hydraulics opened and closed the trunk lid, the power windows, the limousine divider window, the sunroof, and landaulet top, and even the fuel filler door! Front and rear seats were also adjusted hydraulically. The heating and ventilation system included a climate control, which could be set individually for front and rear compartments, and the radio had a remote control allowing the passengers to select the stations and adjust the volume. An intercom was also installed, with a microphone conveniently placed on the steering column so that the chauffeur could respond without removing his hands from the wheel. A total of 13 interior lights kept things well illuminated, especially since the rear compartment had blackout curtains that could be drawn across the rear and side windows for privacy.

Options were limited only by practicality and the buyer's pocketbook. Indeed, where the 600s were concerned, Daimler-Benz spared no expense. Both the long (153.5-inch) and short (126-inch) wheelbase chassis gave the 600 massive proportions. The Limousine's overall length was 18 feet 2 inches, and the Pullman measured 20-1/2 feet. With relatively light curb weights of 5,340–5,731 pounds for the Limousine and 5,820–5,950 pounds for the Pullman, the 6.3-liter powerplant and its accompanying four-speed automatic transmission could propel the cars to speeds well over 120 miles per hour. European versions accelerated from 0 to 60 in anywhere from 9.7 to 12 seconds and covered the standing start quarter-mile in 17 seconds flat.

European road tests recorded top speeds of 129 miles per hour for the Limousine and 124 miles per hour for the Pullman. Revered around the world for its features, quality, and performance, throughout its 18-year production run the Mercedes-Benz 600 was the finest automobile that money could buy—or build.

As the 1960s came to an end, Mercedes-Benz had finally succeeded in establishing itself in North America. The 280 S, 280 SE, and 300 SEL were the most popular models, followed by the high-performance 300 SEL 6.3, sporty 280 SL, 280 SE Coupe and Convertible, and the luxurious 600. Heinz Hoppe's work here was done. In 1970 he would return to Germany and lead the company's expansion throughout Europe. But for Mercedes-Benz and the rest of the world, what the coming decade had in store was something that no one could have anticipated. By 1973 the United States would be mired in a recession. Nixon would be mired in Watergate, and Agnew in tax evasion, leading to both their resignations (Agnew in 1973, Nixon in 1974). Just when things couldn't get much worse, the Arab oil-producing nations embargoed shipments to the United States, Western Europe, and Japan in retaliation for their support of Israel. The embargo precipitated a worldwide energy crisis and virtually crippled U.S. auto sales.

And that was just the beginning.

Interior treatment on the 300 SE and all 300 Series models was exquisite with plush leather upholstery and luxurious wood veneers for the dashboard and instrument pod.

CHAPTER EIGHT

The 1970s and 1980s

Tough Times, Diesel Engines, and New Competition

It was 1970 and the world was in chaos. Of course, if one looks back at the history of the twentieth century, or any century for that matter, the world has always been in chaos. In 1970, however, it seemed to be worse than usual.

The escalating war in Vietnam was testing the conviction of our nation and the free world to fight communism at every step. Moreover, it had emphatically divided America to the point that the National Guard was summoned to Kent State University in Ohio to deal with student protests against the war. This wasn't the first time there had been protests against America's involvement in Vietnam, but it was the first time that shots were fired into a crowd of protesters. In the aftermath of an incident that would galvanize American opinion, the rallying cry of

The 280 SE 3.5 was the last four-seat convertible to come from Daimler-Benz for nearly 25 years. A three-year limited production run of E320 Cabriolets, which concluded in 1997, rekindled the open car theme that today is continued by the new CLK 430 Cabrio.

123

In 1959, Mercedes-Benz began crash testing in an effort to improve driver and passenger safety. The program was under the direction of Béla Barényi, Mercedes' "Father of Passive Safety," who had first proposed the development of "crumple zone" and "rigid passenger cell structure" engineering just prior to World War II. He received patents for both concepts in 1951. *DaimlerChrysler Classic*

the antiwar movement changed from "Hell no, I won't go" to "Four dead in Ohio." Whether or not that was a turning point in our history is likely to be debated ad infinitum, but after Kent State things began to change.

You might wonder what this has to do with Daimler-Benz; actually, quite a lot, because the events of the early 1970s set the stage for one of the most difficult periods in the history of Mercedes-Benz. How Daimler-Benz dealt with the 1970s truly defined the character of the company, especially in the United States, which had become the single most important market outside of Germany.

By 1973 the war in Vietnam was "officially" over, though it really didn't end until the evacuation of U.S. forces, civilians, and refugees in 1975, the year that South Vietnam was overrun by the Communist North Vietnamese. Of course, so much had happened between 1973 and 1975 that Americans had more to be concerned with than the fall of Saigon.

In October 1973, the Organization of Petroleum Exporting Countries (OPEC) had instituted an oil embargo, which led to severe fuel shortages, long lines, short tempers, and big price hikes. Suddenly, people weren't as concerned with how fast their cars could go as they were with how far. Almost overnight the American market for

large, high-performance automobiles evaporated. More and more American consumers were turning toward Japanese imports, feeling that they offered better value, better gas mileage, and higher quality than American cars. This was, for the most part, true at the time. The Japanese imports, compared to European makes like Mercedes-Benz, were also far less expensive. And the problem wasn't just in the United States. The auto industry was in serious trouble on a global scale, because the oil embargo was having an equally devastating effect on foreign economies. Inflation was rampant and economic growth was at a virtual standstill. In the United States, the Dow Jones stock exchange index fell to 663, a number that today seems unfathomable but also helps put the last 30 years in perspective.

With the fuel crisis strangling the U.S. auto industry, the federal government instituted a national 55-mile per hour speed limit in 1974. There would even be a brief period in the 1970s when speedometers were limited to a maximum readout of 85 miles per hour. This was an idea that flew in the face of performance, especially for a company like Mercedes-Benz, which had built its reputation in this country on performance. Federal emission standards were further tightened and automakers were scrambling to build the right cars.

Mercedes-Benz styling in the late 1960s, as this 1967 300 SE shows, had taken on a more formal appearance, as the somewhat ungainly finbacks gave way to the smoother, more rounded lines that would carry Mercedes-Benz styling into the coming decade. *DaimlerChrysler Classic*

A carryover from the late 1960s, the 300 SEL 6.3 was one of the most powerful sedans on the road in the early 1970s, until the new 6.9 arrived. *DaimlerChrysler Classic*

And just when it seemed that smaller, more fuel-efficient models were the salvation, the oil crisis ended.

Gas was freely available once more and prices dropped, although they would never return to preembargo levels. Overall, though, little changed. The 55-miles per hour speed limit still remained, as did new government standards, which were making it harder for automakers to design cars. Most of their R&D money was being allocated to engineering, to meet government regulations that applied equally to imported models.

In 1977 the U.S. Department of Transportation ordered that air bags should be installed in all new cars beginning with the 1982 model year. This presented automakers, who were just figuring out low-impact bumpers, with yet another predicament. To underscore the angst of manufacturers everywhere, the Corporate Average Fuel Economy (CAFE) standard went into effect in 1978. Now, every auto company would have to reach a federally mandated level of average miles per gallon for their product lines. This meant that some

During the 1980s, Mercedes-Benz further developed its diesel engines in response to the world's fuel crisis. Models such as the 300SD grew in popularity throughout this era.

"gas guzzlers" would have to be dropped because they pulled the average down. Then, just to keep things lively, a second fuel crisis hit in 1979, along with a severe recession that finally brought the auto industry to its knees. New car sales slumped as prices rose on the showroom floor, at the pump, and at the bank, where interest rates were soaring.

Despite the economic shallows that were diminishing new car sales, Daimler-Benz had started the 1970s on a very positive note. In the fall of 1969, Mercedes introduced the 280 SE 3.5 Cabriolet, a model that combined the classically inspired styling of the earlier 280 SE with an all-new V-8 engine and the hand-crafted quality that had become a Mercedes trademark. Preserving the regal appearance of Mercedes-Benz Cabriolets dating back to the classic era of the 1930s, the convertible top on the 3.5 folded effortlessly into six layers of cloth, insulation, and padding. When closed, the convertible top was nearly 1-1/2 inches thick, providing superior insulation and soundproofing. With the steel framework concealed from view by a full interior headliner, the manufacturing of each 280 SE 3.5 Cabriolet top required more than 16 hours of hand assembly! Since only 13 cars per week could be built, the Cabriolet was automatically exclusive. Between 1969 and 1971, Daimler-Benz built only 1,232 examples.

Until the arrival of the 280 SE 3.5, the only Mercedes-Benz V-8 available had been the 6.3-liter engine used in the 600 series Limousines and the luxurious 300 SEL 6.3, which were the flagship models of the Daimler-Benz line. Historically, Mercedes had tuned four- and six-cylinder engines for their passenger car lines. Although smaller than the V-8s in many American automobiles, the Daimler-Benz sixes produced nearly the same power by revving much higher, something that would benefit the company well in the troubled years ahead. On the other hand, the new 3.5-liter V-8 was an engineering marvel. Designed using the same performance theory applied to the sixes: "Engine rpm are relatively economical to obtain and are effective if the mixture can be properly controlled by fuel injection," the 3.5 utilized a cast-iron block crowned by aluminum heads and an extremely oversquare combination of 92-millimeter stroke and 65.8-millimeter bore, to achieve a swept volume of 3,499 cc (213.5 ci). With the air-fuel mixture compressed at a ratio of 9.5:1, the fuel-injected single overhead cam V-8 developed a impressive 230 horsepower at 5,800 rpm—more than 1 horsepower per cubic inch—an equation Americans readily understood.

From the very beginning of the 3.5's development, it was clear that the displacement of the V-8 could be easily expanded; and it later evolved into the M117 used to power the 450 SE/SEL models that came into popularity during the late 1970s and 1980s. The 3.5 V-8 also filled the gap between the 3-liter sixes and the 6.3-liter V-8, providing Mercedes-Benz with an entirely new model range. Its modest size and weight allowed the engine to fit the mature 280 SE chassis and provide it with youthful vitality. Despite the Convertible's 110-inch wheelbase, overall length of 196.2 inches, and weight of 3,640 pounds, the 3.5 could arrive at 60 miles per hour from a standstill in 9.3 seconds and reach 130 miles per hour. These were impressive stats for a five-passenger touring car.

The 280 SE 3.5 rode atop a fully independent coil-spring suspension with disc brakes at each wheel, and featured an optional limited-slip differential. Overbuilt in typical Mercedes-Benz fashion, the Convertible avoided the torsional flexing most open cars suffered by using a strengthened chassis with additional steel cross-braces below the leading edge of the rear seat, extending rearward under the trunk. On rough roads, body shudder and cowl shake were virtually nonexistent. Of all

It was the shape that would come to symbolize Mercedes-Benz in the 1970s and 1980s, the magnificent S-Class Sedan. Flagship of the Mercedes-Benz line, the cars carried a variety of engines from high-horsepower V-8s to high-performance diesels.

127

The 280 SE remained in production until 1972, but the six-cylinder models became something of an orphan when the V-8-powered 280 SE 3.5 debuted in 1971. The sporty SE Cabriolets, such as this 1970 model, were among the most beautifully styled cars of the era.

The 280 SE was treated to lavish appointments, leather throughout, including the entire dashboard and instrument binnacle. This example is somewhat unusual in that the original owner ordered the car without a radio. In place of the Becker radio is a 280 SE emblem. The car is also equipped with a manual transmission, so this owner was looking for all-out performance.

Mercedes-Benz models, this was perhaps the quintessential German-engineered luxury touring car. It was also, by nature of its advanced design, capable of meeting U.S. safety standards. In fact, Mercedes exceeded most of the new U.S. regulations before they were even established. This was the legacy of Béla Barényi, the "Father of Passive Safety."

Beginning in 1948, the key principles of passive safety were conceived under the direction of Barényi, who joined Daimler-Benz in 1939. Earlier in his career he had worked at Steyr, alongside Erwin Komenda, later to become Ferdinand Porsche's chief designer, and Karl Wilfert, who left Steyr for Mercedes in 1929 and had since become director of the experimental design department at Sindelfingen. It was Wilfert who brought Barényi into the company just before the war.

His solitary desire since the early days at Steyr had been to build safer cars, and it was Barényi who advanced the theory of "crumple zones." In 1959 he began doing crash tests at Daimler-Benz, which, at the

The 280 SE was powered by an inline six developing 160 horsepower. If an engine could be described as "styled," the 280 SE probably qualified.

"One of the greatest advertising campaigns in Mercedes history was titled 'There Are Times When Mercedes-Benz Almost Wishes It Didn't Have To Be Mercedes-Benz,'" Davis noted. "Bruce McCall, who has written for the leading automotive magazines, and has now become famous both as a comic writer and artist, wrote Mercedes-Benz advertising for the Ogilvy and Mather ad agency from 1965 to 1979. In that capacity, he was the closest thing we had to the great Ted McManus. The mission of those ads was to sell small diesel sedans and fast, luxurious S-class dreadnoughts, of course, but the leitmotif of every ad and commercial was the glory of Mercedes-Benz engineering, or 'overengineering.' McCall worked within the framework of the long-standing David Ogilvy tradition of erudite copy filled with facts large and small. The net effect was months and years of advertising that added up to a veritable encyclopedia of the tremendous trifles that made Mercedes-Benz what it was—the imported luxury car that simply stole the business out from under Cadillac and Lincoln.

"Courting popularity seems to be the main thrust of Mercedes advertising today, and a great deal has been lost, but in the McCall years, Mercedes-Benz in print and on television was both interesting and informative—and very compelling."

Safety measures that might have seemed extravagant to some automakers had become routine to Daimler-Benz by the time Barényi retired in 1972. Mercedes cars were engineered with crumple zones to absorb impact and isolate the passenger compartment in a collision. The fuel tank, all too vulnerable on many automobiles, was surrounded by a metal bulkhead and positioned deep within the body in a protected area over the rear axle. Mercedes doors used tapered cone latches, built to withstand impact and still work. The steering wheel, often criticized for being too large, was designed with a telescoping column and a large padded hub to protect the driver. And the steel passenger shell was developed to protect occupants from side impacts and in the event of a rollover. Thus Mercedes-Benz, along with Volvo and Saab, who followed along similar lines, came to be regarded by consumers as the safest cars one could purchase. In such company the Mercedes were also the best looking.

Styling in the 1970s took another turn in the road and what appeared out of the mist was an entirely new generation of SL roadsters that broadened the appeal of the legendary two-seater even more than had the 230,

time, caused quite a sensation. Barényi was putting ideas to the test that he believed were essential to passenger safety since receiving a patent in 1951 for what was then described as a "rigid passenger cell structure surrounded by front and rear crumple zones." This was followed in 1953 by the self-supporting chassis-body structure with protective side moldings, and a three-part steering column. The overall concept of the passenger cell was finally put into practice with the 1959 Type 220, better known as the "finback" Mercedes. It was to become the forerunner for an entire generation of improved models led by the six cylinder 220, 220 S and 220 SE sedans, coupes, and convertibles.

By the 1960s Barényi's safety program had led to significant progress in passenger protection. Among other things, he had designed the "pagoda" roof for the 230 SL, which was engineered to provide improved all-around visibility and greater structural integrity in the event of a rollover. Head restraints, safety steering column with impact absorber, and padded or rounded-off interior appointments, designed to reduce the injury hazard in an accident, were all visible results of Barényi's influence at Mercedes. The restraint systems were redesigned, too, and the three-point seatbelt became standard on Mercedes-Benz models in the early 1970s.

Passive safety and engineering soon became the hallmark of Mercedes-Benz. And the timing couldn't have been better for the U.S. market. Throughout the troubled decade of the 1970s, Daimler-Benz stressed safety in its advertising, as David E. Davis Jr. wrote in the January 2001 issue of *Car Collector* magazine.

Six cylinders had served the Mercedes-Benz line well since the end of World War II but in 1971 a new V8 joined the lineup: the 3.5 which arrived under the hood of the popular 280 SE. The new 280 SE 3.5 delivered a spirited 200 horsepower.

250, and 280 SL. It was now the 350 SL, 3.5 liters of V-8 power surrounded by an entirely new and even more luxurious body.

Introduced in 1971, the 350 SL was quickly followed by an even more powerful 4.5-liter version, the 450 SL, truly the first Mercedes-Benz sports car to break traditional lines. There was no discrete caste among owners. The 450 SL appealed equally to gray-haired, Brooks Brothers-suited executives on Madison Avenue, and long-haired Levi-clad rock stars on the Sunset Strip, to both men and to women. As a two-seat sports car, this was the Mercedes for all seasons.

In the 350 SL and the 450 SL that followed in 1972, Mercedes-Benz combined for the first time sports car performance and handling with luxury that had previously been reserved for Mercedes touring cars. Historian Richard Langworth described the 350 SL and 450

SL as a sports car "the like of which had rarely been seen by any manufacturer, including D-B itself." In the Unitd States, the bible of American motoring, *Road & Track,* named the 350 SL among the "Ten Best Cars in the World" along with the 300 SEL 6.3 and 280 SE. This dazzling affirmation of the latest Mercedes-Benz models came at a time when it was most needed.

The all-new 350 SL and 450 SL, however different from their gullwinged and pagoda-roofed predecessors, continued traditions established in 1957 with the 300 SL Roadster—the choice of either a fabric convertible top or a removable hardtop; a sweeping open grille with the Mercedes-Benz star and barrel; and seating for just two.

Also known as the Type W 107, the new 350 SL (and 450 SL) chassis measured 96.9 inches, and was greater both in wheelbase and overall length, at 172.4 inches, than the 280 SL. This provided additional interior room to accommodate the installation of air conditioning up front and occasional seating in the rear—the occasion however was limited to small children, pets, an extra suitcase, or some grocery bags. Adults need not apply.

The cars were not only larger in exterior and interior dimensions, but in their structural design and overall weight. The bodies were wider (70-1/2 inches) to accommodate door guard beams federally mandated for the

Daimler-Benz was passing the torch to itself with the 280 SE 3.5 Coupe and Convertible. Both were based on the 220 SE body style, which had been tagged a collector's car by German motoring enthusiasts. *Road & Track* called it "fabulously handsome" and further opined that it was "one of the best-looking body designs to come from any German concern."

American market and to cover wider section tires on a front/rear track of 57.2 and 56.7 inches, respectively. Bodied in steel, rather than aluminum, the new SL weighed in some 350 pounds heavier than its six-cylinder predecessors, yet could clock 0 to 60 miles per hour in an average of 9 seconds, thanks to a potent 190-horsepower 3.5-liter double overhead cam, fuel-injected V-8. When American versions of the 350 SL arrived in 1972, they were already equipped with the new 4.5-liter version of the engine, and these "early" cars were badged 350 SL 4.5. The following year the 350 SL 4.5 was officially rebadged 450 SL. According to one veteran mechanic, "In 1972, when those cars came into the dealership for their first service, we would remove the '350 SL' emblem and replace it with a '450 SL' emblem."[1] American versions came equipped standard with a three-speed automatic transmission. A four-speed automatic was available in Europe, as was a manual gearbox. Unfortunately, neither was offered in the United States because of the changes they effected in emissions. The ultimate 450 SL was the European-only version, which had a robust 225-horsepower output, compared to the emissions-choked 190-horsepower U.S. model.

In America we have a passion for that which we cannot have. Thus, those of wealth and means had to

The smooth backlight and C-pillar styling of the 280 SE 3.5 Coupe was one of the car's greatest features.

Interior of the 280 SE 3.5 was luxuriously appointed and could be ordered with a number of options, including a Becker Europa radio and air conditioning.

horizontal styling of the W 107 body remained in production for another nine years, powered by eight different engines under the designations 280 SL, 300 SL, 350 SL, 380 SL, 420 SL, 450 SL, 500 SL, and 560 SL, leading to an astounding total of 237,287 vehicles sold worldwide between 1970 and 1989, more than all other Daimler, Benz, and Daimler-Benz sports models combined since the company's inception!

The 450 SL Roadster had a companion model in the 450 SLC Coupe, and the line dividing them appeared to be a narrow one. The two cars shared the basic body lines and essentially the same parts, but were intended to appeal to different buyers, and were by design, two very different automobiles.

While the image of the new 450 SL was that of a sports car, the SLC version was designed to be a *gran turismo*. Daimler-Benz had taken a similar approach in the late 1920s with the Model SS Touring and SSK Sports. In the argot of the 1970s, the distinction was between that of a two-seat sports model versus a four-passenger grand touring car designated as a 2+2. The wheelbase of the SLC was 14.2 inches longer than the SL, and the roofline was higher by 1.2 inches to allow more rear seat headroom.

Although the 1971 SLC was introduced with a 3.5-liter V-8 in Europe (it was also later available with a smaller 2.8-liter double overhead cam six and a larger 4.5-liter V-8), the 350 SLC versions that came to the United States in 1972 were actually powered by the 4.5-liter engine in order to meet federal emission requirements and still maintain the performance standards Mercedes-Benz had set down for the car. This was one exception to the displacement of the engine and model name being one and the same. Like the Roadsters, models that arrived at the end of 1972, and all those following throughout the car's history, were rebadged as 450 SLCs. With a price of more than $16,000 (roughly the equivalent of two Cadillacs in 1972), the 450 SLC was regarded as the ultimate in automotive high fashion.

Like the 450 SL, the European version of the SLC was much faster, with a rating of 225 horsepower versus 190 horsepower. Meeting U.S. emissions standards continued to lower the 4.5's performance, and by 1980 output was down to 160 horsepower. Having seen the trend developing, Mercedes-Benz decided that in order to comply with federal regulations, the 4.5-liter engine could no longer be used in U.S. versions and in 1981

have the European version of the 450 SL, and this contributed to an entirely new automotive industry unique to the United States—the gray market. Importers began slipping European-spec 450 SLs into the country and modifying them, for a price, to meet U.S. emissions and safety standards, and the most successful of them were granted authority by the federal government to certify the cars as meeting U.S. standards. An entire book could be written on this great American misadventure.

Arguably the most civilized sports car built up to that time, the Mercedes-Benz 450 SL, became one of the most successful ever, with total production of the 4.5-liter series reaching 66,298 by 1980. The sleek,

Although almost indistinguishable from the standard 450 SEL, the 6.9 models were fitted with slightly larger bumpers than those of other U.S.-equipped Mercedes. Apart from that and the modest 6.9 badge on the trunk lid, all that differed went unseen and unheard. But it was definitely felt when you applied pressure to the accelerator. Powered by a 417-ci V-8, numbers more commonly associated with Detroit muscle cars than luxurious four-door sedans, the 450 SEL 6.9 proved to be the ultimate high-performance luxury car long before other automakers even considered the idea of combining these two antithetical features.

the 450 SL was gone. In its place was a new model, the first "technical" step backward in the company's history since the end of World War II. A 3.8-liter V-8 delivering a maximum of 155-horsepower would now power SL models designated for sale in the United States. Adding to the certain frustration of American buyers who could afford the best was the knowledge that in Europe, there was a 500 SLC 5.0 version pouring out 240 horsepower, and however and whenever they managed to wend their way to America, particularly gray market-rich Southern California, these 5.0-liter models commanded a hefty premium.

Whether a gray market 5.0 or a less powerful 3.8, the consensus about the SLC was the same from just about everybody who owned one. It truly was the best of both worlds. In addition to rousing performance and handling, the SLC offered an unparalleled level of luxury and comfort. Air conditioning, automatic transmission,

power steering, all-disc power brakes, Michelin radial tires, Becker Europa AM/FM stereo, electric antenna, electric windows, central locking system, and a sumptuous leather interior were all standard. With a fully independent suspension, antisway bars front and rear, and virtually neutral steering, they were quick, comfortable, luxurious cars, even the 3.8-liter models. Overall, the SLC was a beautiful piece of work, what every manufacturer of a 2+2 Sports Coupe would have loved to build: the perfect *gran turismo*.

The 450 SL/SLC was among the last designs to come from stylist Karl Wilfert and Mercedes' legendary technical director, Rudolf Uhlenhaut, who retired in 1972. The 450 SL and its variations, which remained in production for an unprecedented 19 years—culminating with the 560 SL in 1989—represent a permanent tribute to Wilfert and Uhlenhaut's legacy of SL models dating from the first 300 SL competition cars in 1952. The five

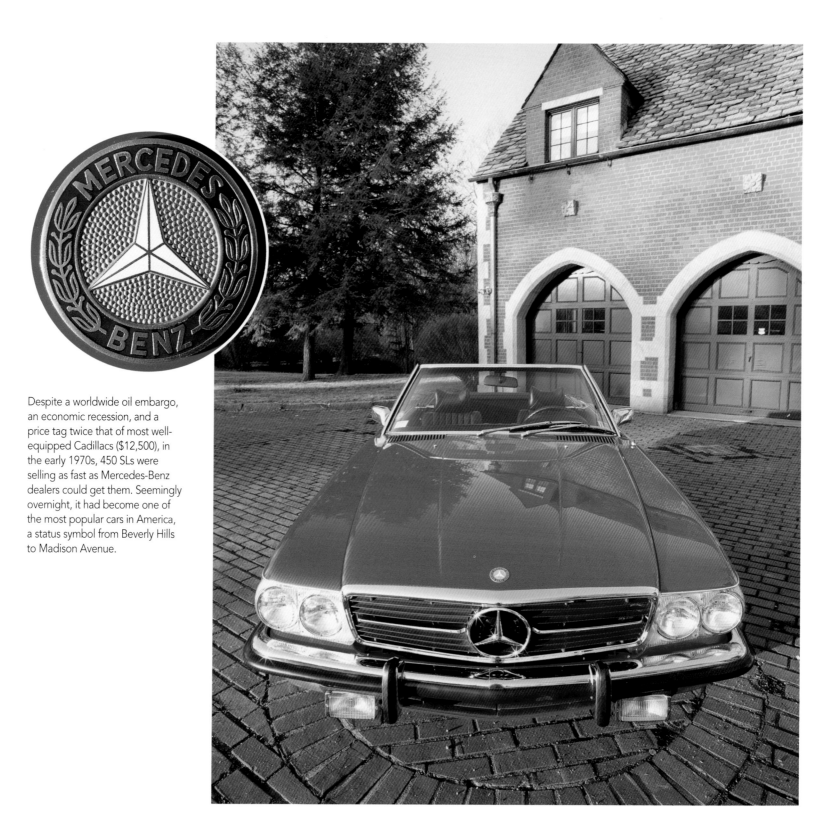

Despite a worldwide oil embargo, an economic recession, and a price tag twice that of most well-equipped Cadillacs ($12,500), in the early 1970s, 450 SLs were selling as fast as Mercedes-Benz dealers could get them. Seemingly overnight, it had become one of the most popular cars in America, a status symbol from Beverly Hills to Madison Avenue.

millionth Mercedes-Benz passenger car of the postwar era (since 1946) was a 1978 450 SLC.

Of course, there was another way to get a more powerful Mercedes in the 1970s—were one willing to forgo the sports car image in favor of what can best be defined as the German equivalent to the American musclecar, the 450 SEL 6.9.

Born of the same philosophy as the earlier 300 SEL 6.3, the 450 SEL 6.9 was a no-holds-barred, cost-be-damned automobile with an engine tuned to meet performance standards. The 6.9 enjoyed one of the largest engines available anywhere. With a bore of 107 millimeters and stroke of 95 millimeters (4.21 inches x 3.74 inches), the 6.9 displaced 6,834 cc, or 417 ci! The 8.0:1 compression engine, even in U.S. trim, developed 360 ft-lb of torque at a remarkably low 2,500 rpm.

Derived from the mighty 6.3 liter V8s that powered the 600 Limousines and 300 SEL 6.3 models, the 6.9's fuel injection system was updated from the Bosch pressure-measuring D-Jetronic to the third generation, mechanically controlled, continuous-injection K-Jetronic, drawing fuel from a copious 25-gallon tank. Dry sump lubrication, which was rarely offered on road cars, was another standard feature of this uncompromising high-performance engine. With better than 280 horsepower (European specifications noted 286 horsepower), the 6.9's stats read more like a Pontiac GTO than a four-door sedan.

Because of its enormous low-rpm strength, the 6.9 was able to get by with a three-speed, torque converter automatic transmission, 2.65:1 rear axle ratio, and limited-slip differential, making the car smoother and quieter, but no less powerful. The suspension was similar to that of the W116 series, but it eschewed coil springs and shock absorbers in favor of an elaborate hydropneumatic springing system. An automatic self-leveling feature compensated for passenger and cargo weight, *(continued on page 141)*

(continued on page 141)

Sleek bodylines, top up or down, gave the 450 SL an elegant, yet sporty appearance that appealed to virtually every age group. It was an ideal blend of sports and luxury car and for 19 years, and with a variety of engines, it remained the most popular sports car design in the world.

Easy-to-read dials and gauges, the largest being the speedometer and tach, were artfully set into the 450 SL dashboard. Mercedes-Benz ads touted "ergonomics" as a key design philosophy long before ergonomics became an industry catch phrase.

The 450 SL was the model that began an SL dynasty. Under the hood of the 1972 to 1980 models was a single overhead cam V-8 with a swept volume of 275.8 ci and an output of 180 horsepower through 1979. The 1980 models had performance lowered to 160 horsepower. The Bosch D or K-Jetronic fuel-injected 4,520-cc engine had a bore and stroke of 92x85 millimeters. The 56 SL was produced from 1985 to 1989 and delivered 227 horsepower from an increased displacement of 5,547 cc or 338.5 ci, with bore x stroke of 96.5x94.8 millimeters.

With the 450 SLC, Mercedes defied American sales tradition. Detroit philosophy had been to offer a list of options as long as a car's wheelbase. Not so Daimler-Benz. The sporty 2+2 model came equipped with virtually every feature as standard equipment. The list included air conditioning, four-wheel disc brakes, automatic transmission, electric windows, a Becker AM/FM stereo, vacuum central door locks, automatic radio antenna, leather interior, radial tires, and styled steel wheels, even a tool kit and a glovebox flashlight.

(Continued from page 137)

keeping headlight aim and bumper height on an even keel. While the system gave a smooth compliant ride, it also took a firm set when driven hard.

Capable of rapid throttle response, a car of the SEL's 116.5-inch wheelbase would normally have been subject to considerable suspension squat under full acceleration and dive under braking, but not so with the 6.9. Two special torque linkages were incorporated into the semi-trailing arm rear suspension, assisted by Watts linkage. Larger diameter front and rear sway bars reduced the 4,400-pound car's body roll in corners. Such advantages were not lost on regular passenger car tires, either. The 6.9 rode on Michelin XWX 215/70VR14 steel-belted radials mounted on 6.5x14 forged light alloy wheels. Although owners seldom became aware of these features, they formed as much a part of the 6.9's substance as its finely tailored leather upholstery and burlwood trim.

Unlike Europeans, Americans had never seen an entry-level Mercedes, but in 1984 they would get their first look at the "Baby Benz," the 190E. Smaller, more affordable, but still a Mercedes, the car quickly became a best seller in the United States. The car was initially offered in the United States with a 2.3-liter gasoline engine developing 113 horsepower (increased to 121 horsepower in 1985), and a less-popular but more fuel-efficient 190 D diesel version. The compact 190 series was offered only as a Sedan, but the cars offered many of the same amenities as the larger Mercedes, including a power sunroof, leather upholstery, and automatic transmission.

The limited edition 190E 2.3-16 sports sedan gave everyone a taste of AMG with ground effects, a rear wing, and a high-performance engine that allowed the cars to, as the model's nickname implied, drop the "Hammer" on the competition.

Ideal for touring the German autobahn at triple digits, on U.S. highways where the maximum was still 55 miles per hour, the 6.9 was perfectly suited to cruising along with the capability of passing anything on the road as the situation demanded, and blowing the doors off so-called musclecars at virtually any speed. Once upon a time, a Pontiac GTO challenged a certain author and an associate who owned a 6.9, late at night on an unmentionable Southern California freeway. Somewhere east of 125 miles per hour the GTO became a pair of headlights growing smaller in the rearview mirror. Such was the 6.9. It had been engineered to be a driver's car, albeit a really big one! Imagine the power of 6.9 liters, capable of moving this boardroom on wheels—one that could accommodate five adults in quiet, comfortable surroundings—from 0 to 60 miles per hour in 8.2 seconds and on to a top speed of 137 miles per hour.

Apart from the more formal 600, the 6.9 was the best of the best, offered to those who would pay upward of $50,000 to purchase one of only 1,816 such cars produced for the U.S. market. In all, Daimler-Benz built

7,380 examples of the 6.9 from September 1975 to May 1980, although sales in this country were limited to the 1978 and 1979 model years. Ringing down the curtain on the 1970s, the 450 SEL 6.9 proved to be an automobile worthy of many superlatives, but needing none.

As the 1970s became the 1980s, little changed in the automotive world. These were still troubled times, and though the gas crisis had passed once again and prices had settled to new norms, consumers were still uncertain about the future and about what kind of automobile belonged in the driveway. Mercedes-Benz would give them a choice unlike any foreign automaker in history. The 1980s was to be the decade of change at Daimler-Benz, one that would see the full implementation of passive safety—ABS (antilock brakes), SRS (supplemental restraint system air bags), traction control, and 4-Matic, Mercedes' first passenger car four-wheel-drive system, introduced at the Frankfurt Auto Show in 1985.[2]

The image Mercedes-Benz had created for itself in the United States was that of a manufacturer of race cars, sports cars, and luxurious touring cars. Americans had little knowledge that Daimler-Benz was the German equivalent of General Motors, with a product line that ranged from off-road vehicles and dump trucks to buses and taxi cabs. To this day, the rows of tan-colored utilitarian-looking Mercedes sedans and wagons outside airports in Frankfurt and Stuttgart are still dismaying to American travelers. After offering such cars throughout Europe since the turn of the century, Daimler-Benz gave North America something that it had never seen in 80 years—an entry-level Mercedes.

The new 190 Series, succeeded by the C-Class, ushered in a new era for Daimler-Benz and brought thousands of new customers into showrooms across the country—people who just a year before could only have dreamed of owning a new Mercedes. Originally introduced in Europe as a new 1983 model, it would take another year before the cars were certified for sale in the United States, but when they arrived Americans were waiting to sign on the dotted line for the new 190E "Baby Benz."

The 190 designation wasn't unique, and in fact, had a rather familiar ring to American sports car enthusiasts who recalled the 190 SL Roadsters sold in the United States from 1954 to 1963. In Europe the 190 series had also included affordable diesel sedans produced in the 1950s and early 1960s. The new 190E seemed nonetheless unusual to Americans. On our shores the last time Mercedes-Benz had offered a car with a 190 designation, LBJ had been in the White House and gas cost 34 cents a gallon! Now it was 20 years later, a gallon of gas took the better part of a dollar, and Ronald Reagan was sitting in the Oval Office for his second term. The C-Class was the right car for the American market in the 1980s, when driving a Mercedes meant that one "had arrived," even if they were arriving in a car that was predominantly used as a taxi cab in Germany.[3] Over time the 190E and 190 D 2.2 (diesel), 190E 2.3, 190E 2.3-16 Sports Sedan and 190E 2.6 variants moved further upscale, becoming more luxurious, and more powerful with the assistance of AMG. Eventually the new C-Class reached the high market status accorded every Mercedes-Benz.

In 1986 Daimler-Benz reached a seminal moment in its history to which no other automaker in the world could ever lay claim. By virtue of the patent received by Karl Benz in 1886, the automobile was officially 100 years old.

By then, economic prosperity had returned, sales were brisk, and there were more Mercedes-Benz automobiles on the road than ever before, from the affordable C-Class, to

AMG-modified high-performance sedans, S-Class Coupes, 300 TE Station Wagons, and sporty 560 SL Roadsters. Prosperity, however, was spreading. There was serious competition from Japanese luxury makes Lexus and Infiniti, and from an ever-improving line of sports and touring cars by BMW. The market that had been almost exclusively dominated by Mercedes-Benz since the 1950s was getting a little crowded.

The 1980s came to a mostly triumphant close, erasing for the most part the financial hardships of the previous 10 years. In 1989 another historic event turned the world's attention toward Germany—the Berlin Wall came down, and the distinction between East and West Germany no longer had any real meaning. This would seem to promise continued prosperity for the coming decade, but as with nearly every turn of the calendar since 1900, events conspired to make the first years of the 1990s troubled ones. The world economy stumbled once more, war in the Middle East captured the headlines again, and an air of political and social uncertainty settled in with the new decade like an unwelcome houseguest.

The roller coaster ride that was the twentieth century continued.

In 1988, Mercedes-Benz introduced the stylish 300 TE station wagon to the United States. Although family wagons had been Mercedes fare for years, the 300 TE marked the first time Daimler-Benz offered a gasoline-powered model in the North American market. Replacing the venerable 300 TD turbo diesel, the 300 TE was powered by a 3.0 liter, 177-horsepower straight six. The same engine used in the 300 E, 300 CE and 300 SEL models of that period. A station wagon of no ordinary means, the 300 TE had the same interior furnishings, engine and handling as the sporty 300 CE Coupe. Priced at $50,000, it was the most expensive station wagon sold in America during the 1980s.

CHAPTER NINE

Modern Times

From the 1990s to the Twenty-First Century

Much had come to pass since Paul Daimler and Wilhelm Maybach built the first Mercedes. Now, as the last decade of the twentieth century began to unfold, there would be a Mercedes-Benz model suitable to virtually every purpose, almost every pocketbook (thanks to the factory-supported Starmark Program established in 1998 for refurbishing and warranting "preowned" Mercedes), and for every field of automotive interest, from sports cars to sport utility vehicles. The 1990s would mark the most ambitious decade in the history of Mercedes-Benz. It would also witness the most extraordinary event since the merger of Benz and Daimler in 1926.

The most significant first-year model of the 1990s was the all-new and long-awaited replacement for the W 107 (450 SL) series, which had been in production for 18 years. Drawing on the historic 300 SL name

The Silver Star legacy is seen in two very different generations of SL, the 1955 SLR and 2000 SLK.

By the early 1990s, the S-Class series included V-8 and V-12 models. Among the best sellers was the eight-cylinder S420 Sedan, which combined exclusive S-Class features with a powerful engine and a price under $80,000.

for the first time in more than 30 years, Daimler-Benz focused on the image of the great Gullwings and Roadsters from the 1950s and 1960s, with the beautifully styled six-cylinder 300 SL in 1990, followed in 1991 by the eight-cylinder 500 SL. The new cars introduced a litany of improvements over their 450 SL-derived predecessors, including an automatic top that completely disappeared beneath a solid boot. Once again the stylists at Daimler-Benz had created a seemingly timeless design, although it was the engineering department that

would have the most sway with the stylish new sports cars throughout the 1990s.

When the 1995 SL models were introduced, they marked the beginning of a new era in Mercedes-Benz marketing. The cars were little changed in appearance, but the names and audience at which they were directed certainly were. There was a clear division among the models now designated SL320, SL500, and SL600—putting the letters before the numbers for the first time—and distinctly dividing the line into three

categories: 6-, 8-, and 12-cylinder models, respectively, with styling similar to the 1990 AMG version of the car, which featured more pronounced front and decklid spoilers, side skirts, and rear valance.

Mechanically, AMG tuning for the SL in 1990 had offered a number of options, including a new rear differential gear set, which changed ratios from 2.65 to 3.27 and cut better than a half-second off 0–60 times. AMG sport exhaust systems added 7 to 8 horsepower, and the ultimate option—a 6-liter "exchange" motor—delivered 381 horsepower, compared to the stock 5-liter's 322 horsepower. An AMG-powered 500 SL could run from 0 to 60 in five seconds flat. It could also break the bank. The new 6-liter engine, including the trade-in allowance of the stock 5-liter, was an estimated $25,000. The body treatment, rear differential, wheels, and tires added another $18,000. For the privilege of making Porsches and Ferraris eat Daimler dust, SL owners paid up to $45,000 above the $91,000 base price for a 500 SL in 1990. Five years later, buyers would pay six figures for the factory's ultimate SL, the

The S500 provided the highest level of luxury with a V-8. The next step up was the V-12 S600 and a price in the six-figure range.

In 2000 the S-Class was completely revised with new styling, slightly smaller dimensions, and a full range of engines. The sweptback styling influence first seen on the new E-Class had finally evolved into a new generation of Mercedes-Benz design for the twenty-first century.

Today's versions of the SL320, SL500, and SL600 incorporate AMG-like treatments on the exterior. All three versions are equipped with a fully automatic convertible top that lowers the windows, raises the tonneau, retracts the top, and closes the tonneau with the touch of a single button. And when you put the top up, the automatic mechanism even remembers to close the windows!

Popular in Europe, the A-Class Mercedes is regarded as a subcompact, although it offers exceptional cargo and passenger capacity. It is possible that an upscale version of the A-Class may find its way to the U.S. market in the coming years as a fuel-efficient entry-level Mercedes-Benz model.

high-performance V-12 SL600. Mercedes-Benz had, in a way, undone what the 450 SL had achieved with its universal appeal and price. The new SLs established an economical and performance caste that separated owners of the $78,300 six-cylinder Mercedes SL320 from those who purchased the V-8 SL500 priced at $89,000 and V-12 SL600, which commanded $120,100. Where only a few options and AMG treatments had differentiated W 107 models throughout the series, the SL was now for the first time divided by performance and price.

The greatest changes at Daimler-Benz, however, had begun back in 1993, when Mercedes introduced the all-new E-Class as a midrange sedan model. Developed in response to the Lexus and Infiniti luxury lines from Toyota and Nissan, and to the midrange BMWs, all of which were beginning to take market share from Mercedes, the E-Class leveled the playing field in one swift move and created an entirely new segment of Mercedes owners. But this was just the beginning. After only three years, the E-Class was completely revised for 1996. Filling the shoes of the best-selling Mercedes-Benz model ever would seem

no mean feat, but Daimler-Benz handily succeeded in this benchmark with an even better E-Class line that finally accomplished what no previous model had, to combine the luxury and style of an S-Class with the size and practicality of a midsized model. Not since the 220 SE of the late 1950s and legendary 300 SE of the 1960s had Mercedes-Benz offered so much in an automobile.

The E320 at $43,500 was more car than anyone should have reasonably expected for the money in 1996, a price that was some five percent *less* than the model it replaced! The sweeping bodylines of the E320 gave it a powerful stance more reminiscent of a sports coupe than a four-door sedan. Unique in appearance from the laid-back headlight design to the wraparound rear lighting array, the car introduced a new style that set it apart from any other Mercedes-Benz model. It was a design guaranteed to evoke a reaction. And that it did. Gone from the E-Class were the last vestiges of that old Teutonic frost of flat textures and sterile surfaces. The E320 offered the warmth and character of a Jaguar Saloon with stylishly contoured surfaces and contrasting color schemes. The car's innovative side

The latest SLK delivers supercharged performance from a 3.2-liter, 215-horsepower V-6.

Mercedes-Benz 2001

ollowing the introduction of an all-new S-Class in 2000, Mercedes-Benz celebrates the 100th anniversary of the Mercedes brand name in 2001 with the greatest product range in the company's 115-year history, including an all-new C-Class.

The world's oldest automaker now offers passenger vehicles that are comprehensively equipped with innovative safety and luxury features. Many of the standard safety features, in fact, were industry "firsts." All 2001 Mercedes-Benz passenger vehicles sold in the United States are equipped as standard with the following safety features: Electronic Stability Program, Tele Aid, Supplemental Restraint System (three-point seatbelts with Emergency Tensioning Retractors in front, dual front air bags, front door–mounted side air bags and knee bolsters), ASR full-range traction control, ABS antilock brakes, Brake Assist (reduces stopping distance in panic stops), BabySmart child seat detection system, theft deterrent system with remote door locking, climate control, power windows, cruise control, AM/FM/weatherband/cassette audio system, Flexible Service System, integrated garage door opener, and free scheduled maintenance for the vehicle warranty period of four years or 50,000 miles.

The following chart outlines the latest cars to bear the Mercedes-Benz name.

C-Class Sedans

Vehicle type: Midsize sport Sedan
Wheelbase: 106.9 in.
Length: 178.3 in.
Weight: 3,219–3,285 lbs.

- All-New C240 Sedan ($29,900) with 168-hp, 2.6-liter V-6.
- All-New C320 Sedan ($36,950) with 215-hp, 3.2-liter V-6.
- All-new models for 2001 established class-leading value and luxury, and feature cutting-edge design inspired by the new S-Class Sedans. Standard equipment includes a new six-speed manual for C240 and Touch Shift for C240 and C320 automatics, Tele Aid, and Electronic Stability Program (ESP).
- Competitors: Audi A4, BMW 3-Series, Cadillac Catera, Infiniti I30, Lexus ES300 and IS300, Volvo S70.
- Key standard features: front air bags, door-mounted side air bags in front and rear, side head protection curtains, adjustable multifunction display and steering wheel, Tele Aid, leather seat inserts, front and rear express-up and down power windows, auto-dimming rearview and driver side-view mirrors; SmartKey remote locking and antitheft system.

E-Class Sedans and Wagon

Vehicle type: Full-size luxury Sedans and Wagon
Wheelbase: 111.5 in.
Length: 189.4 in.
Weight: 3,680–3,955 lbs.

- E320 Sedan ($47,850) and Wagon ($48,650) with 221-hp, 3.2-liter V-6.
- E430 Sedan ($53,200) with 275-hp, 4.3-liter V-8.
- E55 Sedan ($70,300) with 349-hp, 5.5-liter V-8.
- The popular E-Class sets a continuing benchmark of quality, safety, and value. Current generation E-Class introduced in 1995 as 1996 model and received substantial updates for 2000 model year. The E55 AMG performance model was added in 1999.
- 4MATIC all-wheel-drive available for E320 Sedan, E320 Wagon, and E430 Sedan ($50,700, $51,500, and $56,050, respectively).
- Competitors: Audi A6, BMW 5-Series, Cadillac Seville, Infiniti Q45, Lexus GS300, GS400, and LS400.
- Key standard features: Electronic Stability Program (ESP), Tele Aid, side air bags front and rear, multifunction steering wheel, Touch Shift manual control for automatic transmission, side head protection curtains, 10-way power front seats with three-position memory, leather seat surfaces (full leather on E320, E430, and E55 Sedans).

S-Class Sedans

Vehicle type: Premium luxury Sedans
Wheelbase: 121.5 in.
Length: 203.1 in.
Weight: 4,133 lbs.

- S430 ($70,800) with 275-hp, 4.3-liter V-8.
- S500 ($78,950) with 302-hp, 5.0-liter V-8.
- New S55 (price not yet available) with 354-hp, 5.5-liter V-8.
- New S600 ($114,000) with 362-hp, 5.8-liter V-12.
- All-new S-Class introduced in 1999 as 2000 model; new S600 debuts an all-new V-12 engine, ABC active suspension; new S55 marks the first AMG-produced S-Class, debuts high-performance 5.5-liter V-8 in the S-Class, features ABC active suspension.
- Competitors: Audi A8, BMW 7-Series.
- Key standard features: side head protection curtains, rear side air bags, electronic air suspension with adaptive damping, Nappa leather interior, COMAND (COckpit MANagement and Data system) with integrated GPS Navigation, Bose audio system, laminated side glass, hydraulic door and trunk closing assists; S55 adds 354-hp, 5.5-liter V-8, ABC active suspension, AMG aerodynamic package, 18-inch AMG performance wheel/tire package; S600 adds 362-hp V-12 engine with Active Cylinder Control, Parktronic, additional wood trim, four-zone climate control, CD changer, and integrated digital Motorola Timeport cell phone with voice recognition software, unique 17-inch wheels.

SLK-Class Coupe/Roadster

Vehicle type: 2-seat Coupe/Roadster
Wheelbase: 94.5 in.
Length: 157.9 in.
Weight: 3,055–3,099 lbs.

- Facelifted SLK230 Kompressor ($38,900) with 190-hp, super-charged/intercooled 2.3-liter four-cylinder engine.
- New SLK320 ($43,900) with 215-hp, 3.2-liter V-6.
- Fully automatic retractable hardtop.
- Exterior and interior facelift in April 2000 for 2001 model year. New SLK320 model features a 215-hp V-6; SLK230 Kompressor receives power increase to 190 hp. For both models, new six-speed manual is standard.
- Competitors: BMW Z3 2.8, Porsche Boxster.
- Key standard features: leather upholstery, Bose sound system, telescoping steering column, headlamp washers, antitheft system.

M-Class Sport Utility Vehicle

Vehicle type: Sport utility
Wheelbase: 111.0 in.
Length: 180.6 in.
Weight: 4,510–4,653 lbs.

- ML320 with 215-hp, 3.2-liter V-6.
- ML430 with 268-hp, 4.3-liter V-8.
- ML55 AMG with 342-hp, 5.5-liter V-8.
- Award-winning SUV combines Mercedes-Benz passenger car safety, quality, performance and comfort. Full-time four-wheel drive, four-wheel electronic traction control and four-wheel independent suspension. Introduced fall 1997 as 1998; ML430 for 1999; ML55 AMG for 2000.
- Competitors: Infiniti QX30, Land Rover Discovery II, Lexus RX300, BMW X5.
- Key standard features: Electronic Stability Program (ESP), Tele Aid, dual-stage front air bags, door-mounted side airbags, new Downhill Traction System, antitheft system, burl walnut trim, leather steering wheel, 80-watt audio system. ML430 adds leather upholstery, 17-inch wheels, GPS Navigation. ML55 AMG adds 18-inch wheels, four-piston front brake calipers, glass sunroof, Xenon headlamps, unique bodywork and leather, seven-speaker 150-watt audio system.

CLK-Class Coupes and Cabriolets

Vehicle type: Luxury/performance Coupes and Convertibles
Wheelbase: 105.9 in.
Length: 180.2 in.
Weight: 3,213–3,665 lbs.

- CLK320 Coupe ($41,950) with 215-hp, 3.2-liter V-6.
- CLK320 Cabriolet ($48,900) with 215-hp, 3.2-liter V-6.
- CLK430 Coupe ($49,650) with 275-hp, 4.3-liter V-8 and Sport Package.
- CLK430 Cabriolet ($56,500) with 275-hp, 4.3-liter V-8 and Sport Package.
- New CLK55 AMG ($67,400) with 342-hp, 5.5-liter V-8
- Introduced in 1998. CLK320 Cabriolet and CLK430 Coupe introduced for 1999, CLK430 Cabriolet for 2000.

- Competitors: BMW 3-Series Coupes and Convertibles, Lexus SC300 and SC400 Coupes, Volvo C70 Coupe and Convertible.
- Key standard features: ESP (Electronic Stability Program), Tele Aid with enhanced functions, multifunction steering wheel, Touch Shift, leather upholstery, Bose audio system, insulated power top (Cabriolet), revised SmartKey with remote locking and antitheft system.

SL-Class Coupe/Roadsters

Vehicle type: 2-seat Roadsters
Wheelbase: 99.0 in.
Length: 177.1 in.
Weight: 4,121–4,473 lbs.

- SL500 ($83,800) with 302-hp, 5.0-liter V-8.
- SL600 ($128,950) with 389-hp 6.0-liter V-12.
- Current generation introduced in 1989 as 1990 model.
- New enhanced aerodynamic package as standard equipment, one-touch convertible top and removable aluminum hardtop standard for both. Glass Panorama roof and Sport Package optional for both.
- Competitors: Jaguar XK8 Convertible, Porsche 911 Carrera Cabriolet.
- Key standard features: Electronic Stability Program (ESP), automatically deploying rollbar system, Tele Aid, Nappa leather interior, Bose sound system.

CL-Class Coupe

Vehicle type: Premium luxury Coupe
Wheelbase: 113.6 in.
Length: 196.6 in.
Weight: 4,115 lbs. (est.)

- CL500 ($87,500) with 302-hp, 5.0-liter V-8.
- CL55 with 354-hp, 5.5-liter V-8.
- CL600 ($117,200) with 362-hp, 5.8-liter V-12.
- Introduced in 2000, offering the finest luxury, comfort, materials, and a previously impossible ride/handling combination from Active Body Control (ABC) active suspension; high level of advanced materials to minimize weight.
- Competitors: Bentley Continental, Jaguar XK8.
- Key standard features: ABC active suspension (counteracts body roll, dive, squat), Electronic Stability Program (ESP), COMAND (COckpit MANagement and Data system) with on-board navigation, Bose audio system with CD changer, multifunction steering wheel; CL55 adds 354-hp V-8 engine, AMG aerodynamic enhancements, unique 18-inch wheel-tire package; CL600 adds 362-hp V-12 engine with Active Cylinder Control, integrated digital Motorola Timeport cell phone with voice recognition, unique 17-inch wheels.

continued on next page

What lies ahead for Mercedes-Benz? Within the next few years we can expect to see a new super car based on the Vision SLR concept, a stunning design for a two-seater, that also hints at performance and safety technology Mercedes-Benz could offer in future vehicles.

The new design study blends futuristic styling from the current Mercedes Formula One World Champion Silver Arrow race car with classic design elements from the famous Mercedes SL sports car and SLR racer of the 1950s. The evocative design of its arrow-shaped front end is based on the Formula One race car that Mika Häkkinen drove to victory in the 1998 World Championship. These race car design cues also appear in the cockpit and along the body.

The long chiseled hood, sweeping fender lines, and unique doors hearken back to the 1950s 300 SL sports car and its SLR racing version, which legendary drivers such as Juan Manuel Fangio, Rudolf Caracciola, and Stirling Moss piloted to numerous victories.

The dramatic look of the SLR design study incorporates a double spoiler across the front of the car and a new interpretation of the familiar Mercedes-Benz "face," featuring four oval headlights. The body is formed with lightweight fiber-reinforced materials and aluminum.

A 5.5-liter supercharged version of the twin-spark/three-valve Mercedes-Benz V-8 engine produces more than 550 horsepower and about 530 ft-lb of peak torque. This advanced powerplant gives the SLR Vision truly staggering performance: 0–60 in about 4-seconds, 0–125 miles per hour in just over 11 seconds, and a top speed of 200 miles per hour .

The technology that stops the Vision SLR is no less exciting than the technology that makes it go. A new electro-hydraulic brake system calculates brake pressure for each wheel, relying on input from a variety of sensors, including information on traction and stability. The result is quicker response from the brake pedal, optimum braking stability when cornering in wet conditions, and compensation for fade on any individual brake.

The brake discs also represent a leap in technology. Instead of conventional cast-iron, the discs are made from fiber-reinforced ceramics. Not only are these brake discs 67 percent lighter than conventional discs, they can handle twice the temperature load—up to 2,900 degrees Fahrenheit.

Inside, the Vision SLR features an all-new concept for a sports car cockpit, dominated by a wide, gently curving console. Instead of a conventional instrument panel, the SLR Vision has a "spoiler" housing two classic-looking instruments. Likewise, the oval steering wheel breaks from convention and offers the driver an unfettered view of the instruments. Function and comfort are ensured by lightweight carbon-fiber bucket seats.

Some of the features used in the Vision are already available, such as the Cockpit Data and Management system (COMAND), which is standard equipment on the all-new Mercedes S-Class. From COMAND, the driver can access the on-board satellite navigation system, as well as controls for the audio and phone systems.

While the Mercedes-Benz Vision SLR is only a concept vehicle, a production version is expected in the not-too-distant future. Not far off either, is the likelihood that an edition of the subcompact A-Class sold in Europe will find its way to the United States as the ultimate entry level Mercedes.

As the twenty-first century unfolds, new technology and an even greater diversity of products may one day bridge the gap that has separated Americans from some of the most exciting automobiles sold in the world.

A century after the first car to bear the name appeared—it seems we may have once again "entered the Mercedes era."

With the hardtop raised, the SLK becomes a two-passenger sports coupe. In 25 seconds, the car can be converted, at the touch of a button, into an open roadster.

impact supplemental restraint system also added to the interior design by necessitating a textured door panel that resembled gathered leather, very much in the idiom of British and Italian luxury car interiors. Achieving new levels of luxury, performance, and safety, the E320 established a new standard for midclass models. A Mercedes-Benz that doesn't cost a fortune but looks and drives as if it should!

The next surprise that Daimler-Benz sprung was a new sports car, not a replacement for the SL, but a lower-priced companion model, the SLK.

It had been a long time coming. More than 30 years. That was the last time Mercedes-Benz offered a low-price sports car powered by a four-cylinder engine. That was the 190 SL, and when it vanished from the road in 1963, so too did the concept of a small, sporty two-seater from Stuttgart.

In 1998, Mercedes-Benz rekindled the 190 SL's flames but with a car that burns so much brighter. Powered by a double overhead cam, four-valve-per-cylinder engine paired with its Roots-type supercharger, the SLK was the first supercharged Mercedes-Benz production car since 1939! Thus the SLK deserves considerable attention here. It plays on all the same themes as the 190

PREVIOUS PAGE:
At the other end of the spectrum, future plans at DaimlerChrysler call for the production of the ultra luxury Mercedes-Benz Maybach, which will be a competitor to Rolls-Royce and Bentley. The Maybach name dates back to Daimler's partner, Wilhelm Maybach. Maybach resigned from DMG in the early 1900s and after World War I established his own auto company. Maybach was acquired by Daimler-Benz in the 1960s. The twenty-first century luxury car will bring full circle the Daimler-Maybach legacy.

The second series E-Class redefined the midsize luxury market and brought a new generation of owners into Mercedes-Benz showrooms.

SL—an ideal combination of compact size, modest but pleasing performance, and all-weather practicality. But the SLK goes one step further. While the 190 SL, and all Mercedes-Benz roadsters since the first 300 SL, offered a removable hard top, there was always one problem—where to put it. Most sat on furniture pads when not in use or hung from the garage ceiling. And it was never convenient to remove or attach the hardtop. The SLK solution, though hardly ingenious, offered the best alternative in Mercedes-Benz history. The hard top would simply fold up automatically and store away in the trunk at the touch of a button. Perhaps it was ingenious, because that feature made the SLK the most innovative sports car Mercedes-Benz had ever built.

The SLK roof was and still is absolutely fascinating from the moment the rear decklid lifts and the top rises up and away from the windshield, until it settles quietly into the trunk. It takes only 25 seconds. You can do it at a stoplight and stop traffic. With the top raised, the SLK is a coupe—solid, secure, and fully protected from the elements. There isn't the faintest trace of wind noise, no compromise in the car's aerodynamics. No

hint from inside that this is a convertible. The idea that one can have it both ways, convertible when the weather suits and hardtop when it does not, makes this a *practical sports car*—three words which rarely appear in the same sentence.

Substantially shorter than the SL, the SLK is a true two-seater and there is nothing behind driver and passenger but bulkhead. While there is more than ample leg, shoulder, and head room in the cockpit, the Mercedes-Benz designers didn't plan on SLK owners taking any long trips. Trunk space with the top lowered is at a premium. There is a pull-out divider in the trunk (like a window shade) that clips into a sensor lockout. This defines the usable cargo area in the trunk, whatever you can get below the divider. If you are going to lower the top, it acts as an interlock to prevent the hardtop from coming down if it is not in place, and a large suitcase is.

Mercedes-Benz stylists excelled with exterior design, giving the SLK a sense of proportion that stands alone top up or down. And while creating a completely new design, they were careful to retain traditional, if not historic characteristics—the grille opening that has

represented the SL lineage for more than 40 years, and on the hood a classic reprise of the twin power domes of the 300 SL. But what they did on the inside was even more impressive.

We spend our time behind the wheel, not on the outside admiring the fender lines. When you slip into the driver seat of the SLK, it is wide, with better sidelong support than big SLs offer. All of the controls fall at hand, almost in a second nature fashion, they seem to be where you would expect them; nothing clever or innovative, just a straightforward driver's cockpit. The design is 1950s retro combined with 1990s carbon fiber; a curving dashboard binnacle and instruments that are a stand-out design rimmed in

chrome with attractively back-lighted ivory faces and black numerals. Everything else is grouped in the center console, the hand brake recessed alongside the driver seat. It is a dynamic juxtaposition of timeless design and modern technology.

The car handles easily, and unless you really press, it is difficult to push the rear end out. With ABS braking and ASR traction control, the SLK hasn't any bad habits. It is suitably balanced for the power available and the engine provides just enough agility to make driving fun. The AMG version takes it just a little further. Also more than up to the task are the brakes, adapted from the larger E-Class. Although most of the SLK's underpinnings are C-Class derived, the engineers reasoned,

A Mercedes-Benz sport utility vehicle might have seemed unlikely in the 1970s and 1980s, but in the 1990s it not only became a reality with the 1998 ML320, but it was built in the United States.

157

For 2001, Mercedes-Benz introduced an all-new C-Class with the up-market styling of the flagship S-Class.

and rightly so, that putting the E-Class binders on a lighter-weight car like the SLK would deliver exceptional braking capability.

The SLK is a true sports car, cut from the same legendary cloth as the 190 SL, the MGA, Jaguar XK-120, and Porsche 356, a fabric that has not been so finely woven in decades. This car is fun to drive, fast enough through the gears, responsive enough when pushed hard into a corner, yet comfortable enough to sustain you though freeway traffic when speed is no longer a factor. It is in the real world of day-to-day life where the SLK proves itself. Pull into a parking lot, push a button, and 30 seconds later you're locking the door on a hardtop coupe. Such virtues, original or not, can't be denied.

The SLK had plenty of company in 1998, giving Daimler-Benz the most diversified product line since the 1930s, when there were Mercedes models in virtually every price range and classification from economical

The 2001 CLK Cabriolet combines E-Class styling with high performance in either the 215-horsepower 3.2-liter V-6 CLK320 or 4.3-liter 275-horsepower V-8 CLK430.

diesel sedans to luxurious touring cars. Customers could now chose from C-Class, E-Class, and S-Class, from sedans, sporty CLK coupes, and cabriolets, and E-Class station wagons, to SL and SLK sports cars, a selection of AMG-modified sedans, and a sport utility vehicle—the ML320—the first Mercedes-Benz to be built in the United States since the American Mercedes in 1905.

Unless one spent a great deal of time in Germany, four-wheel-drive sport utility vehicles with silver star hood ornaments were unheard of in the United States. Unlike past Mercedes-Benz SUVs, which were exclusive to the European market and more in the Land Rover vein, the ML320 was not only going to be available in the United States, it was also going to be built there, in a new assembly plant located in Tuscaloosa, Alabama.

The very image of a modern sport utility—what Mercedes-Benz prefers to call an All-Activity-Vehicle—the M Class brought something new to the table, the versatility of an off-road vehicle with the refinement, integrity, and luxury image of a Mercedes-Benz. The M Class was designed with the American market in mind, or in other words, to cater to the needs of customers who think they need a four-wheel-drive vehicle, whether they do or not. For the most part this is a tall Mercedes sedan with folding rear seats and the capability to tackle snow and mud, and to ford flooded roads with the agility of a Jeep. It's also luxurious enough to drive to the country club. The ride is more car-like than truck-like, and the interior is pure Mercedes-Benz, subtle textures and colors, well-placed gauges and controls. Think of it as a tougher version of a car, exactly what would have been expected from Mercedes-Benz.

With the 1998 model line it seemed there was nothing left undone, but even all this would pale in comparison to the biggest merger in automotive history. On May 7, 1998 Daimler-Benz formally announced its plans for the amalgamation of Daimler-Benz AG with Chrysler Corporation, creating an international conglomerate—DaimlerChrysler AG. The new company came into being on November 17 when the first share was traded at the New York Stock Exchange. This was a stunning, historic move both for Daimler-Benz and Chrysler, two companies that appeared to be doing quite well on their own. Underlying the merger, however, was a deep seeded desire each company had for change. Chrysler had the most forward thinking design studio in the U.S. and Mercedes had brought engineering and

technology to new heights. Daimler-Benz needed more dealers in the U.S., Chrysler more in Europe. It was a marriage not of necessity, as had been the merger of Daimler and Benz in 1926, but one of mutual admiration. Both Chrysler and Daimler-Benz stood to benefit in countless ways. With DaimlerChrysler AG comes an exchange of information, technology and design that will lead to a remarkable generation of Chrysler and Mercedes-Benz products in the twenty-first century.

One of the greatest changes at Daimler-Benz, however, had begun back in 1993, when Mercedes introduced the E-Class as a mid-range sedan model. In part, a response to the Lexus and Infiniti luxury lines from Toyota and Nissan, and to the mid-range BMWs, all of which were beginning to take market share from Mercedes, the E-Class leveled the playing field in one swift move and created an entirely new segment of Mercedes owners. But this was just the beginning. After only three years the E-Class was completely revised for 1996. Filling the shoes of the best-selling Mercedes-Benz model ever would seem no mean feat, but Daimler-Benz handily succeeded in this benchmark with an even better E-Class line that finally accomplished what no previous model had, to combine the luxury and style of an S-Class with the size and practicality of a mid-sized model. Not since the 220 SE of the late 1950s and legendary 300 SE of the 1960s, had Mercedes-Benz offered so much in an automobile.

One wonders what Walter Chrysler, Gottlieb Daimler, and Karl Benz would have to say.

The CL-Class premium luxury Coupes are available with a choice of 302-horsepower 5.0-liter V-8, 354-horsepower 5.5-liter V-8, or 362-horsepower 5.8-liter V-12.

CHAPTER TEN

A History of Mercedes-Benz Racing

The Masters of Road and Track

Т he motor sport history of Mercedes-Benz is a story of success. No matter whether you look at the nineteenth, twentieth, or twenty-first century, racing cars from Stuttgart have
always been, and continue to be, in the top league in sporting competition. Countless racing victories—from the
world's first car race in 1894 to Mika Häkkinen's Formula 1 World
Championship titles in 1998 and 1999 with McLaren Mercedes—testify
to perfect race car engineering, the drivers' unflagging determination to
win, and the development of efficient teamwork.

More than 100 years of motor sport under the three-pointed star re-
flect the origins of motor racing as well as the breathtaking speed at

The Sauber-Mercedes race cars were further developed for the 1989 season in
technical terms—a new V-8 biturbo engine with four-valve technology had a peak
output of 925 horsepower—and in their livery. Their silver-colored paintwork
unmistakably signaled that Mercedes-Benz was back on the track. In keeping with
their heritage, the new Silver Arrows won 16 out of the 18 races in 1989 and 1990,
including the 24 Hours of Le Mans in 1989. *DaimlerChrysler Classic*

The first major racing triumph for Mercedes was the 1903 Gordon Bennett race in Ireland, won by Belgian race driver Camille "Red Devil" Jenatzy in a Mercedes 90. *DaimlerChrysler Classic*

which the engineering of the successful Mercedes-Benz racing cars developed. [1]

The history of motor sports is truly as old as the motorcar itself. Although conceived by Gottlieb Daimler, Wilhelm Maybach, and Karl Benz as a means of personal transportation, it wasn't long until courageous men came up with the idea of competing against each other in the first motorized vehicles. The world's first car race in 1894 marked the beginning not only of motor sport but also of automotive engineering development at a breathtaking speed. Manufacturers quickly become aware of the publicity effect

motor racing success could have, and began to promote the sales of their road-going vehicles through competitive triumphs. It was the birth of the "Win on Sunday, Sell on Monday" philosophy.

In the first official effort of pitting one motorcar against another—the international race from Paris to Rouen—the cars finishing in the first four places were powered by Panhard-Levassor engines that were built to the Daimler principle. These V-2 units developed 3.5 horsepower and permitted the cars to cover the 125-kilometer route at an average speed of 20.5 kilometers per hour, or at a breathtaking speed, for the time, of 12 miles per hour. In the following years, vehicles with Daimler engines continued in this vein, clinching numerous victories and consolidating the good reputation of top-class engineering from Germany. The first victory of a Daimler car from Cannstatt, entered by Allgemeine Motorwagen-Gesellschaft, in a race from Berlin to Leipzig and back to Berlin, occurred in 1898.

The turn of the century marked the beginning of dynamic development, away from the previous carriage-type

vehicle and towards the automobile, as we know it today. The sensational breakthrough was achieved at a surprisingly early stage, in 1900, when Wilhelm Maybach built a pioneering car for the 1901 Nice race week, powered by a 5.9 litre four-cylinder engine installed at the front, developing a remarkable 35 horsepower and providing the car with a top speed of 86 kilometers per hour, a truly monumental speed for the time. It is attributable to Emil Jellinek that this modern car is regarded as the first "Mercedes."

From that point forward, the Mercedes name has been at the forefront of motor sports competition for 100 years. As early as 1903, the unrelenting search for ever better automobiles led to the 60-horsepower Mercedes, at whose wheel the Belgian Camille Jenatzy—one of the first professional racing drivers in history—clinched a major international success for the Cannstatt-based company—victory in the legendary Gordon Bennett race in Ireland, the first major triumph for Mercedes.

A big fire destroyed almost the entire production facilities of the first DMG factory in Cannstatt, forcing Daimler to move to new premises in Untertürkheim in 1904, one year earlier than planned. Sadly, the new 90-horsepower racing cars, which were to be entered in the next Gordon Bennett race, also fell victim to the flames. It was the company's first racing disaster.

Other highlights before World War I were the successes of Daimler and Benz in the French Grand Prix—an event in which "la Grande Nation" in 1908 had actually wanted to prove that the fastest racing cars were French—but the laurels all went to Germany. A first and a fifth place for the 140-horsepower Mercedes cars and second and third ranks for the racing cars of Benz & Cie. in Mannheim impressively proved the superior qualities of the German brands. Innumerable victories and respectable finishes in road and hillclimb races followed in the years before the outbreak of World War I, including a repeat triumph in the 1914 French Grand Prix. On a racetrack near Lyon, Christian Lautenschlager, Louis Wagner, and Otto Salzer scored an uncontested 1-2-3 victory in cars called "Mercedes 115 horsepower 4.5-liter Grand Prix." It took the victorious Mercedes drivers a little over seven hours to complete the 752.6 kilometer

race—at an average speed of no less than 105 kilometers per hour—better than a mile a minute.

Neither Mercedes nor Benz officially participated in motor sport competitions during World War I and for two years afterward. The success story was continued by individual drivers at the wheel of German cars, such as American Ralph de Palma, who won the 1915 Indianapolis 500 in a Mercedes Grand Prix racing car.

Three years after World War I, motor sport competition was revived in Germany and other countries. Otto Salzer, Max Sailer, and once again, Christian Lautenschlager were the Mercedes company drivers who were able to keep numerous competitors at bay in European hillclimbs and road races in 1921. Their cars were further developed Mercedes versions of the 1914

In the post–World War I years, both Benz and Daimler made advances in race car design. In 1923 the revolutionary aerodynamic rear-engine Benz "teardrop" appeared in the very first race in Monza, and virtually untried, finished a respectable fourth place, along with winning a special prize for the "most unusual" racing car of all competitors.
DaimlerChrysler Classic

One of the legendary drivers of the 1920s and 1930s, Rudolf Caracciola brought Daimler-Benz an unprecedented number of championship victories during the greatest era in motor sport history.
DaimlerChrysler Classic

Grand Prix and mighty aero-engined 28/95-horsepower Mercedes. [2]

In the early 1920s, the design offices of Daimler-Motoren-Gesellschaft had turned their attention toward the development of supercharged racing engines. Gottlieb Daimler's son, Paul, who had taken over as chief engineer after Wilhelm Maybach's withdrawal in 1907, encouraged their development. DMG engineers had plenty of experience in mechanical supercharging at their disposal—as superchargers had already been used to boost the power of Daimler aircraft engines during World War I.

In 1922 a 1.5-liter and 2.0-liter displacement formula was introduced. Paul Daimler developed a completely new 1,500-cc supercharged four-cylinder engine with two overhead camshafts, driven by a vertical shaft and operating four valves per cylinder. The first race in which the new 6/40/65-horsepower model appeared was the Targa Florio in Sicily. Company driver Paul Scheef competed in the 1.5-liter class and finished a respectable third place. At the wheel of another supercharged car with a 140-horsepower engine, Max Sailer clinched the

If not the most charismatic of prewar Mercedes-Benz drivers, then certainly the longest living— Manfred von Brauchitsch is 96 years old and still getting around under his own steam. He appeared at the first Mercedes-Benz Classic Days in Salzburg, Austria, in September 2000, to retell how he drove his Mercedes-Benz SS to victory in the 1929 Gaisberg Rennen hill climb. During his career with Daimler-Benz, which officially began in 1934, when Alfred Neubauer hired him as a factory driver, but started as a privateer in 1929, von Brauchitsch stood in the winner's circle no fewer than 45 times by 1939.
DaimlerChrysler Classic

With all of the paint scraped off and the body polished to its aluminum surface, the W 25 with von Brauchitsch at the wheel, went on to win the first 750-kilogram formula event in the 1934 Eifelrennan at the Nürburgring.
DaimlerChrysler Classic

first victory for a supercharged automobile in the class over 4.5 liters. It was Sailer's first attempt.

At the same time, a spectacular if not revolutionary racer was created at Benz in Mannheim—the teardrop car. It was both the systematically aerodynamic shape and the location of the engine, behind the driver, that caused such a sensation. In engineering and styling terms, the new Benz racing car was clearly modeled on the famous Rumpler teardrop-shaped car. Victory in the very first race in Monza in September 1923 was not to be expected, but Fernando Minoia's fourth place and a special prize for the "most unusual" racing car of all competitors, ranked as an undisputed *succès d' estime*.

The original version of this interesting car was not entered in any other races—due in part to the economic crisis in post–World War I Germany and in part to the cooperation between Mannheim-based Benz & Cie. and Untertürkheim-based Daimler-Motoren-Gesellschaft, which began in 1924 and culminated in the merger of the two companies into Daimler-Benz Aktiengesellschaft (D-B AG) on June 28, 1926. During this transitional period, racing activities were first and foremost initiated by DMG.

Once again, the European Grand Prix in Monza was the stage for the spectacular debut of a new racing car from Stuttgart. Everybody's eyes were drawn to the grim-looking radiator design of the 2-liter Grand Prix cars in their white livery. Behind the vertically mounted radiator, a completely new supercharged straight-eight-cylinder engine generated an output of 170 horsepower. Ferdinand Porsche, who had left Austro-Daimler to become new chief engineer at DMG following Paul Daimler's departure, developed the engine. Also new to DMG was a young race driver named Alfred Neubauer, cutting his teeth behind the wheel of one of the four eight-cylinder Mercedes. In later years, Neubauer was to become the legendary racing manager of Daimler-Benz.

Monza, however, was not the right place for the new cars. After just a few tests, they did not have the required level of maturity for victory in 1924. But two years later, the supercharged eight-cylinder Mercedes-Benz secured an important win in the first German Grand Prix on the Avus in Berlin. Rudolf Caracciola, just 25 years old at the time, together with his codriver Otto Salzer, not only clinched a hotly contested victory but also reached an average speed of over 85 miles per hour, thought to be virtually impossible in those days.

The promising supercharging of the 2-liter Grand Prix car was further developed for the next generation of Mercedes-Benz sports cars, the models K, S, SS, SSK, and SSKL, all of which but the SSKL were created under the guidance of Ferdinand Porsche. In contrast to the previously used thoroughbred racing cars, the new models had also been designed as sporty road-going cars. Popularly known as "white elephants" between 1926 and 1933, for DMG's factory racing colors, and powered by supercharged six-cylinder engines, these cars were the measure of all things on both normal roads and racetracks anywhere in the world. They were just the right "tools" for well-to-do drivers to pit themselves against each other in all manner of gentlemanly racing competition, which in the 1920s and 1930s were regarded as social events of the highest order.

In 1927, Daimler-Benz cars competed in more than 90 races and other motor sport events. The models K and S were the first to cross the finishing line on countless occasions—hillclimb races, automotive tournaments, circuit races, you name it. One of the most outstanding triumphs to this day is the triple victory in the opening race on the Nürburgring on June 19,

1927, when Rudolf Caracciola won this race ahead of Adolf Rosenberger and von Mosch across the finish line. Caracciola and Rosenberger both drove 1.9-ton Mercedes-Benz S models with mighty 6.8-liter engines. With the supercharger engaged, this engine generated 180 horsepower at 3,000 rpm.

The engineers' and designers' untiring striving for perfection produced the SS model, which replaced the Mercedes-Benz S in 1928. It differed from its predecessor mainly in that it had a revised, more powerful engine, which, in the racing version, generated up to 250 horsepower. In the German Grand Prix on the Nürburgring, the Mercedes-Benz company team secured a much-acclaimed 1-2-3 victory—the winner was Rudolf Caracciola ahead of Otto Merz and Christian Werner.

In 1929 a young German race driver named Manfred von Brauchitsch drove an SS up the Gaisberg in the inaugural Austrian hillclimb outside Salzburg. His performance would later earn him a place on the Mercedes-Benz race team in 1934. Now 96 years old, von Brauchitsch is the last remaining member of the original Silver Arrow team from the 1930s.

The victors in 1939 with the W 154 were Hermann Lang, Rudolf Caracciola, and Manfred von Brauchitsch. *DaimlerChrysler Classic*

The W 125 and driver Rudolf Caracciola totally dominated European racing up until the beginning of World War II. *DaimlerChrysler Classic*

Driving the SSK and SSKL, Rudolf Caracciola claimed victory after victory during the late 1920s and early 1930s and acquired worldwide fame, at the same time underlining the extraordinary qualities of the racing sports cars from Stuttgart. The last evolution of the awe-inspiring Mercedes-Benz SSKL was entered in the Avus race in Berlin in 1932 and driven by privateer Manfred von Brauchitsch, who had the car fitted with streamlined bodywork, just the competitive edge he needed to defeat Rudolf Caracciola, who was driving for Alfa Romeo at the time.[3]

The fame accumulated by all these successes in motor racing also benefited sales in Germany and abroad. The advertising department of Daimler-Benz AG exploited the victories to the full. Prominent people throughout the world—among them Prince Max zu Schaumburg-Lippe, Prince Esterhazy, Count Carlo Felice Trossi, and actress Lilian Harvey—all succumbed to the charm of the large supercharged Mercedes cars and numbered among the glamorous Mercedes customers of that time.

Even though the large supercharged Mercedes cars scored victory after victory, their time seemed to be running out. As early as 1932, the international motor racing authority, AIACR, decided to introduce the 750-kilogram formula (weight without fuel, oil, coolants, and tires). This weight limit was not to be exceeded.

The officials intended to ban the ever larger, ever more powerful, and ever heavier cars from the racetracks for safety reasons, since their handling had become difficult, especially with regard to brakes and tires. The new weight restrictions came into force in 1934. In spite of the economic crisis, which affected all motor manufacturers, Daimler-Benz had developed the W 25, a car to become legendary at a later stage, to meet the specifications. The W 25's eight-cylinder inline engine with supercharger and four-valve technology developed 314 horsepower from a displacement of 3.36 liters. Equally progressive was the car's running gear, with four-wheel independent suspension and hydraulically operated drum brakes.

The legend of the Silver Arrows was created in the W 25's very first race under the 750-kilogram formula on the Nürburgring. Despite its systematic lightweight design, the car was still 1 kilogram above the limit, and it was no longer possible to incorporate technical modifications during the night before the June 3, 1934, race. Faced with the certainty that the W 25 would not be able to qualify, driver Manfred von Brauchitsch whispered to racing manager Alfred Neubauer, "You'll just have to think up one of your old tricks, or else sitting here watching the race will be like watching paint dry!" It was that remark which prompted Neubauer to have all of the white paint scraped off of the W 25's body, and the car polished down to its bare aluminum finish. The weight of the paint had been 1 kilogram! Thus the Silver Arrows were born in 1934 and von Brauchitsch went on to win the Eifel race in record time.

Strong competition from the Auto Union—their cars were, incidentally, later nicknamed "Silverfish"— eventually prompted the further development of the highly successful W 25. In the course of the years, the eight-cylinder's displacement increased from 4.0 to 4.7 liters, and the engine developed up to 494 horsepower, depending on the type of supercharger and fuel quality.

In the Roadster configuration, the 300 SL race cars dominated the 1952 Nürburgring event, finishing first through third in the sports car races.
DaimlerChrysler Classic

The only loss the 300 SLs experienced was in the most grueling of European road races, the Mille Miglia. Team Manager Alfred Neubauer made up for the disappointment later in the year by sending his cars into the toughest road race in the world, the Carrera PanAmericana, where the Mercedes took the checkered flag to conclude their record-setting 1952 season.
DaimlerChrysler Classic

The 1935 season was an extraordinarily successful one for Mercedes-Benz. The company team won 9 out of 10 races with the W 25 and scored 5 double victories; Rudolf Caracciola won the European and German champions' titles, and the battle with Auto Union for the world speed record attracted international attention.

In 1936, Alfred Neubauer's team finally found its masters in the company teams of the Auto Union and Alfa Romeo. The W 25 only won a handful of individual races that year and it appeared the Silver Arrow had lost its dominance. Enter Rudolf Uhlenhaut.

The experience gained against the newly fortified competitors suggested a restructuring of the racing department—young Rudolf Uhlenhaut became chief engineer, and from his analyses of the W 25, the W 125 emerged a year later. The chassis was modified more extensively than the supercharged eight-cylinder engine. For weight reasons, the idea of a completely new V-12 was abandoned again, and the proven inline engine was thoroughly revised in terms of displacement, carburetor, and supercharger. The engines now generated up to 646 horsepower from a displacement of almost 5.7

From 1955, American driver Paul O'Shea won three successive titles—twice at the wheel of a 300 SL Coupe and once, in 1957, in a 300 SLS.
DaimlerChrysler Classic

Neubauer added a young Englishman, Stirling Moss, who was accomplished both in Formula 1 and sports car racing, to the Mercedes-Benz team. His greatest victory was the 1955 Mille Miglia in which he and codriver Denis Jenkinson set a record with the 300 SLR that has never been broken.
DaimlerChrysler Classic

per hour) in the final heat; the top speed of 380 kilometers per hour (228 miles per hour) in this race was not to be exceeded until 1959!

Ever more powerful and ever faster, in the course of just a few years, the 750-kilogram formula racing cars had reached ever-new heights. With output ratings of more than 650 horsepower and top speeds of over 400 kilometers per hour (240 miles per hour) in record runs, safety and reason called for a scaling down of engine performance. Thus came the 3-liter formula limiting the displacement of supercharged engines to 3 liters and that of engines without superchargers to 4.5 liters. Daimler-Benz retained the supercharger principle and developed the W 154. The new, further developed car was based on the W 125 but powered by a completely new V-12 with a cylinder angle of 60 degrees, developing 430 horsepower in its initial form. It is interesting to note that all the new 3-liter cars were faster than the clearly more powerful racing cars entered the previous year! The first major triumph with the W 154 was accomplished by the Mercedes-Benz team in Tripoli/Libya when Hermann Lang, Manfred von Brauchitsch, and Rudolf Caracciola scored a fantastic triple victory. Against strong competition from Maserati, Alfa Romeo, Bugatti, and Auto Union, Caracciola won the 1938 European champion's title for the Stuttgart-based team.

After having won six races, the W 154 was systematically further developed for the 1939 season. In its further improved chassis, the V-12 now developed 480 horsepower. It was another exciting season with numerous Mercedes-Benz victories, culminating in three titles: the European champion's and German hillclimb

Two of the greatest men in Mercedes-Benz racing history, Alfred Neubauer congratulates driver Juan Manuel Fangio after he clinched the 1955 Formula 1 world champion's title. *DaimlerChrysler Classic*

liters. With the W 125, Mercedes-Benz was again a big step ahead of all the other manufacturers in 1937. Rudolf Caracciola regained the German championship as well as the European champion's title, but the highlight in this ever-so-successful year for Mercedes-Benz was, without any doubt, the international Avus race. Hermann Lang, who had been promoted from racing mechanic to company driver, reached an uncontested average speed of 261.7 kilometers per hour (157 miles

As rare today as a 300 SLR, the custom-built factory car carrier used to transport the race cars. Note the famous SLR air brake in its deployed position. *DaimlerChrysler Classic*

champion's titles went to Hermann Lang; Rudolf Caracciola won the 1939 German road race championship.

What no doubt stunned everyone in 1939, however, was the response of Mercedes-Benz to rule changes in the Tripoli Grand Prix. The Silver Arrows had won in 1935, 1937, and 1938, but for 1939 it was to be staged for 1.5-liter racing cars exclusively. Rumor had it that the organizers wanted to give the Italian manufacturers a chance to win; the marked dominance of Auto Union and Daimler-Benz in the 3-liter formula races is not unlikely to have played a role. However, in the unbelievably short time of eight months, Uhlenhaut and his designers developed a 1.5-liter car for this race: the W 165. Its supercharged V-8 engine developed a remarkable 254 horsepower. After just a single test a few days before the event, racing manager Alfred Neubauer's team sent out Rudolf Caracciola and Hermann Lang to race against a superior lineup of 28 Italian and British racing cars. Daimler-Benz succeeded in once again proving its excellence with a stunning double victory. Lang won the race ahead of Caracciola; the third-ranking Alfa Romeo was one lap behind when it crossed the finish line.

The W 165 was not entered in any other races in 1939 because those responsible held the view that it would otherwise devalue the regular 3-liter formula for Grand Prix cars. With a record that seemed unassailable, Mercedes was preparing for the 1940 season when the outbreak of World War II forced all racing activities to be curtailed. It was the end of an era for Daimler-Benz.

By the end of World War II, nearly 80 percent of the plant facilities in Stuttgart-Untertürkheim were destroyed. The first priority was to reconstruct the plant in order to resume industrial activity, and nobody seriously thought of resuming motor sport activities, except one man: Alfred Neubauer. He searched for 3-liter Mercedes racing cars in working condition, and found them. And so the company set out to compete in motor racing again in 1951, entering three refurbished W 154s in the race in Buenos Aires, Argentina. Alongside doyen Hermann Lang, the factory team now included Karl Kling and the Argentinean Juan Manuel Fangio. The three company-entered Mercedes-Benz cars finished the *Premio Presidente de la Nación Juan D. Perón* race in second, third, and sixth places, with Lang ahead of Fangio and Kling. However respectable, the result could not belie the fact that the 12-year-old W 154 was getting on in years; all formula racing plans were therefore stopped for the time being. Instead, Daimler-Benz now set its sights on being competitive again with a racing car utilizing a 2.5-liter naturally aspirated engine specified by the International Racing Commission,

Fangio and the new 2.5-liter W 196 Streamliner competing in the 1955 race at Monza. *DaimlerChrysler Classic*

acclaim. After 24 hours, the team of Hermann Lang/Fritz Riess was the first to cross the finish line, followed by their teammates Theo Helfrich/Helmut Niedermayr. The 300 SL again occupied the first three places in the sports car race on the Nürburgring.

The cars had virtually swept the 1952 racing season, but Neubauer had one more event on his mind. He decided to put the 300 SL to the ultimate test, the competition in the Carrera PanAmericana: 1,941 miles

Not every race was won by a 300 SL or SLR. In the 1959 Algiers-Cape Rally, the winner was a 190 D diesel driven by Karl Kling and Raner Günzler. *DaimlerChrysler Classic*

Driving a slightly modified production 230 SL, Eugen Böhringer and Klaus Kaiser won the 1963 Liège-Sofia-Liège rally, proving that the new SL was made of the same stuff as the legendary 300 SL.. *DaimlerChrysler Classic*

FIA. In addition, a promising sports car series was launched in which Daimler-Benz competed throughout 1952 with a revolutionary new race car, the 300 SL.

The 300 SL, developed by Rudolf Uhlenhaut, Fritz Nallinger, Karl Wilfert, and their respective engineering and design teams, was first entered in the classic Italian long-distance race, the Mille Miglia. Karl Kling fought a long duel with a Ferrari before being forced to let it pass due to technical problems on his own car. In the next race, in Berne, Switzerland, Mercedes drivers Kling, Lang, and Riess scored an outstanding triple victory. Rudolf Caracciola was out in the lead for some time, but crashed against a tree after experiencing brake problems. The most famous racing driver of the prewar era did recover from this accident, but his career as a racing driver was over.

The double Mercedes victory in the classic long-distance race in Le Mans attracted enormous public

The "finback" cars made a name for themselves in competition as well. Here a 1962 Sedan is seen in the Argentine road race. *DaimlerChrysler Classic*

174

over Mexican roads, part of them unpaved, at icy-cold altitudes and through muggy lowlands. It would be a test for both man and machine. The team of Kling/Klenk experienced its greatest adrenaline rush when a vulture hit the windscreen at over 120 miles per hour and ended up, torn to pieces, inside the car! The fact that the team was nevertheless the first to see the checkered flag testified not only to the 300 SL's superiority but also to the excellence and intrepidity of drivers Karl Kling and Hans Klenk. With the victorious 300 SL, Mercedes-Benz proved that the company was able to continue its magnificent prewar successes. Next would be a return of the Silver Arrows to Formula 1 racing in 1954.

In 1953 the Daimler-Benz racing department was busy preparing for the new Formula 1. A completely new car with a 2.5-liter naturally aspirated engine was developed: the W 196. It was built with three different wheelbase lengths, as a monoposto, and with streamlined bodywork. The tubular grid frame had been adopted from the 300 SL sports car and the engine developed for this model was again an eight-cylinder inline unit—the first to feature direct fuel injection and desmodromic valve control. Its output was 265 horsepower initially and 290 horsepower at a later stage. The naturally aspirated unit was able to rev up to 9,000 rpm.

Racing manager Alfred Neubauer's team took the return to Grand Prix racing very seriously indeed, as shown in its very first race. Karl Kling and Juan Manuel Fangio in their brand-new W 196 cars already dominated the practice sessions for the French Grand Prix in Reims on July 4, 1954. In the race itself, they didn't give their competitors with Ferrari, Maserati, Giordini, and HWM a chance, scoring a much-acclaimed double victory, with Fangio finishing ahead of Kling.

Other victories during that season included Kling, Fangio, and Hermann finishing in order in the Avus race in Berlin. The 1954 season culminated with Juan Manuel Fangio winning the world champion's title in a Mercedes-Benz W 196.

Parallel to its activities with the revised W 196 racing cars in Formula 1, Mercedes-Benz set out in 1955 on a successful course with 300 SL touring cars and the newly developed 300 SLR racing sports cars. Company drivers now included Juan Manuel Fangio, Karl Kling, and Hans Herrmann as well as Englishman Stirling Moss and the Italian driver Piero Taruffi.

A 1960 "finback" heads to victory in the Acropolis Rally. *DaimlerChrysler Classic*

The first race in the 1955 Formula 1 season was staged in Argentina and after a three-hour battle in scorching heat, Fangio was the first to cross the finishing line. His teammate, Stirling Moss, won his first race at the wheel of a W 196 on home ground, in Aintree. The competitors had a hard time of it because the Stuttgart team's drivers Fangio, Kling, and Taruffi finished in superior fashion claiming second, third, and fourth places in England. At the end of the season, Fangio had amassed the largest number of points and clinched the 1955 Formula 1 world champion's title ahead of Moss. However, the plucky Englishman more than made up for it with the 300 SLR.

Driving a 300 SLR with start number 722, Moss celebrated a memorable victory on April 30, 1955, when with codriver Denis Jenkinson he won the Mille Miglia in 10 hours, 7 minutes, and 48 seconds, at an average speed of better than 100 miles per hour, a record that has remained unsurpassed to this day!

The incident with the most serious consequences in the company's motor sport history occurred on June 11, 1955, in the 24-hour race in Le Mans. French driver Pierre Levegh was involved in an accident through no fault of his own and his 300 SLR was catapulted into the crowds. The tragic death of numerous spectators prompted those responsible at Mercedes-Benz to withdraw all drivers from racing.

Daimler-Benz had been considering a withdrawal from racing for some time and following the tragedy at *Circuit de La Sarthe*, the company announced its complete withdrawal from motor sport on October 22, 1955. Another era had come to an end at the pinnacle

In 1905, Wilhelm Maybach, when asked what he thought was the optimal number of cylinders, replied: "One cylinder would be best, two cylinders are just about tolerable, four cylinders are too many and six cylinders are not worth discussing." Despite this, just one year later he designed Daimler's first six-cylinder engine and fitted it in this racing car. The engine was an inspiration for many later aircraft engines. The 1906 race car had an output of 120 horsepower and a top speed of 90 miles per hour.

of success. In all those years, the team around racing manager Alfred Neubauer had not only provided for thrilling races but had also demonstrated that victory requires more than just fast cars and drivers. The Neubauer era, which had begun as early as 1926, can safely be credited with marking the beginning of team-work, superior pit work, and perfect racing strategy.

After the company's withdrawal from Formula 1 and sports car racing, Mercedes-Benz cars were entered in rallies by private teams. Rallies were first and foremost an acid test of the reliability of what were slightly modi-fied production cars. After Alfred Neubauer's retirement, ex-racing driver Karl Kling was appointed sports director and assumed responsibility for the support the company provided in selected motor sport events.

In the late 1950s and early 1960s, the six-cylinder-engined 220 SE and 300 SE Saloons and the 300 SL sports cars became very much a talking point along the

Sometimes less was more, as in the case of the 1924 supercharged Mercedes Targa Florio race car powered by a four-cylinder engine delivering 120 horsepower. The car's convincing win in the Targa Florio race in 1924 was the sensation of the year. Supercharging had come of age.

roads and dirt tracks of the world. In 1956 the team of Walter Schock/Rolf Moll won the European rally championship. An unusual victory was achieved by the team of Kling/Günzler in the 14,000-kilometer Mediterrannée-Le Cap rally in 1959, driving a Mercedes-Benz 190 D. One year later, it was again the team of Schock/Moll that secured the European rally championship for itself in a 220 SE: they were the first to cross the finishing line in both the legendary Monte Carlo Rally and the Acropolis Rally in Greece.

In the following years, up until 1964, company and private drivers won numerous rallies and races in their fast "fin tail" Mercedes cars, as this model was lovingly nicknamed. Among the top-ranking names in the winner's lists were Schock/Moll, Kling/Günzler as well as Eugen Böhringer, Lang, Knoll, Eger, Glemser and Braungart and, time and again, Ewy

This was the last of the 750-kilogram formula cars and a vehicle of superlatives. Although it was used in racing for only one year, it allowed Mercedes-Benz drivers to mount the winner's stand on 27 occasions!

After winning all but their first race in 1952, the 300 SL Mercedes were sent to Mexico to compete in the toughest road race of them all, the Carrera PanAmericana. The car pictured, which has been superbly restored for display in the Mercedes-Benz Museum, was driven to victory by Karl Kling. The bars welded over the windshield were added in Mexico after a vulture crashed through the windshield.

The W 196 R Streamliner was built for Formula 1 racing when the new requirements came into force in 1954, stipulating a maximum capacity of 2.5 liters for unsupercharged cars. Juan Fangio and Karl Kling drove the cars to a 1-2 finish in the 1954 French Grand Prix.

The interior of the 300 SLR was pure race car, but executed in a sporty fashion that would have been suitable for a production car. The noise level inside the SLR Coupe, however, was deafening, as anyone who has ever ridden in it will attest.

Rosqvist and Ursula Wirth, the only women to drive for Mercedes-Benz.

The Mercedes-Benz 300 SLS was specially designed for the American sports car championship. The car was based on the 300 SL production sports car and converted into a highly competitive car for this series by reducing its weight to 970 kilograms and boosting its power output from 215 to 235 horsepower. Beginning in 1955, American race driver Paul O'Shea won three successive titles—twice at the wheel of a 300 SL Coupe and once, in 1957, in a 300 SLS.

Another highly competitive car of this era was the 230 SL. It was in this car that Böhringer/Kaiser

clinched a much-acclaimed victory in the Liège-Sofia-Liège marathon rally in 1963.

Throughout the 1960s and 1970s a variety of Mercedes-Benz models were campaigned by privateer racers, particularly in the new 450 SL. In 1980, Daimler-Benz competed in all races of the rally world championship with 300-horsepower 500 SLC cars. Against tough competition, the teams of Waldeggard/Thorszelius and Recalde/Streimel scored a double victory in the Bandama rally at the end of the season. This was the last success of a company-supported team in rally racing. In December 1980, the board of management of Daimler-Benz AG decided to withdraw from the world championship for capacity reasons.

The numerous victories over many years of rally sport competition by what were nearly stock production cars demonstrated the reliability of Mercedes-Benz automobiles to potential customers and to millions of television spectators throughout the world who came to recognize the Mercedes-Benz name.

In 1984, Daimler-Benz set out once again to become actively involved in international motor sport. Several private teams, among them AMG, entered the 190E 2.3-16 in the Group A championship in 1986. Volker Weidler clinched the runner-up title in the very first season; Roland Asch repeated this success in 1988. A year later, the Mercedes-Benz 190E was developed

The most famous 300 SLR design was the 1955 Gullwing Coupe built for Rudolf Uhlenhaut. A Formula 1 racing car for the road, this was one of two such cars built with lines modeled on the production 300 SL Coupe. Uhlenhaut put more than 10,000 miles on the test car driving from race to race in Europe and arriving usually ahead of the team, just to unnerve the competition with the dramatically styled F1 road car.

179

The greatest of the 300 SLR race cars was number 722, driven by Stirling Moss to a record speed victory in the 1955 Mille Miglia. This marked the heyday of the legendary 300 SLR Silver Arrows. Both the Moss and Uhlenhaut 300 SLRs are restored and on display in the Mercedes-Benz Museum in Stuttgart.

into the 2.5-16 versions, equipped with a 330-horsepower engine. The next evolution stage was triggered in 1990: the four-valve four-cylinder engine now had an output of 373 horsepower. The fast Mercedes touring cars often emerged as the winners in exciting races against tough competition from Audi, BMW, and Opel. In 1991, Daimler-Benz's endeavors bore fruit: the company won the manufacturers' title and Klaus Ludwig the runner-up title.

The Mercedes team dominated the touring car championship in 1992 and won the team ranking; Klaus Ludwig clinched the drivers' title. In its last year, 1993, the 190E 2.5-16 secured the runner-up title for Roland Asch.

In 1994 the new Mercedes C-Class entered the motor sport stage. Its 2.5-liter six-cylinder engine developed over 400 horsepower in its first season. Klaus Ludwig and Jörg van Ommen took the champion's and runner-up titles, respectively, and Mercedes-Benz won the manufacturers' ranking. In 1995 the new ITC (International Touring Car Series) was staged in parallel with the DTM. Both series were won in superior

Group A Motor Sport Mercedes take to the field in the 1994 Hockenheim. The new C-Class racing cars were powered by a 2.5-liter six-cylinder engine that developed over 400 horsepower. Klaus Ludwig and Jörg van Ommen clinched the champion's and runner-up titles and Mercedes-Benz won the manufacturers' ranking.
DaimlerChrysler Classic

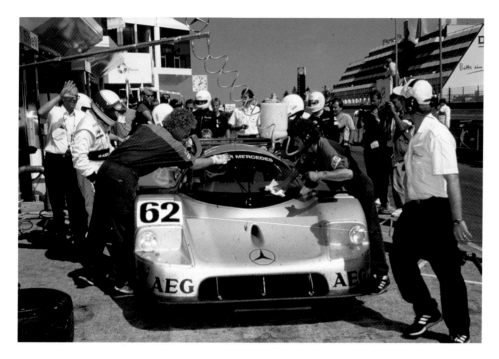

fashion by AMG driver Bernd Schneider, and in both series, Mercedes-Benz came away with the manufacturers' titles.

Between 1986 and 1996, Mercedes-Benz became the most successful brand in DTM/ITC racing with its fast 190E and C-class racing cars. In the end, the brand had recorded 84 victories, 4 driver championship titles, 5 manufacturers' titles, and 10 runner-up positions in the manufacturers' rankings.

Between 1985 and 1987, Daimler-Benz supported the Swiss Sauber team with V-8 engines for the team's Group C sports cars. In 1988 the Swabian manufacturer with the long-standing tradition again entered a company team and won five races with the 700-horsepower Sauber-Mercedes C 9.

The Sauber-Mercedes race cars were further developed for the 1989 season not only in technical terms— a new V-8 biturbo engine with four-valve technology had a peak output of 925 horsepower—but also changed livery. Their silver-colored paintwork unmistakably signaled that Mercedes-Benz was back on the

Of the 19 starts that the great Sauber-Mercedes made in 1989, only two failed to finish in a season that saw Sauber-Mercedes establish complete dominance of Group C.
DaimlerChrysler Classic

The McLaren-Mercedes of David Coulthard in the 1999 season. The West McLaren-Mercedes team won the Grand Prix World Championship for Manufacturers, and driver Mika Häkkinen won the FIA Formula 1 World Championship for drivers.
DaimlerChrysler Classic

track. In keeping with their heritage, the new Silver Arrows won 16 out of the 18 races in 1989 and 1990, including the 24 Hours of Le Mans in 1989.

In 1990 the Mercedes C 11—as the cars were meanwhile called—clinched the runner-up title. It was the year in which the Mercedes-Benz junior team was founded, with drivers Michael Schumacher, Heinz-Harald Frentzen, and Karl Wendlinger. The regulations were changed in 1991: supercharged engines were no longer permitted and displacement was limited to 3.5 liters. In compliance with these new regulations, the new Mercedes-Benz C 291 powered by a V-12 engine was built. Plagued by technical defects, the C 291 won only one race—the last race of the season in Japan, and the winners were Michael Schumacher and Karl Wendlinger.

After withdrawing from Group C racing, Daimler-Benz and the Sauber team jointly looked for a new challenge in international motor sport—and found it in the Formula 1 world championship. Almost 40 years after its withdrawal from Formula 1, Mercedes-Benz returned in 1994 as an engine partner to a Formula 1 team. After a lengthy barren period, Mercedes-Benz and Sauber went their different ways in 1994. Since then, McLaren has been the new partner in the tough Formula 1 business. The British team with its long-standing tradition and unrestrained determination to win is the most successful in Formula 1 history to date. The two partners' fruitful cooperation culminated in the constructors' title in 1998 and two drivers' titles for Mika Häkkinen, in 1998 and in 1999. History continues to be made.

World Sports Car Championship series Mercedes-Benz CLK-GTR. A street version of the car was also available at a cool $1.5 million a copy!
DaimlerChrysler Classic

CHAPTER ELEVEN

The Mercedes-Benz Museum and Classic Center

Where Past and Present Are One

Unlike any automotive museum in the world, the complete history of the automobile is illustrated by means of one and the same make in the Mercedes-Benz Museum. The oldest automobile company in the world was always at the forefront of development, beginning with the first two automobiles, the Benz Patent Motorwagen and Daimler Motor Carriage, through the first Mercedes and the racing and record-breaking cars of the twentieth century to the high-technology vehicles of today.

The foundations of the present collection were created when the automobile was still in its infancy. Various original items were preserved, at both the Daimler-Motoren-Gesellschaft and at Benz & Cie., for the purpose of design studies and patent research. DMG had an exhibition of

The center of the museum is a maze of ramps that climb three flights, each lined with historic cars from Mercedes, Benz, and Daimler-Benz.

185

Rebuilt for the 100th anniversary of the automobile in 1986, the Mercedes-Benz Museum in Stuttgart is the only museum in the world where the entire history of the motorcar can be traced from its inception. The stunning glass structure has a skylight ceiling that allows the cars to be illuminated by natural light.

Race cars dominate the ramps and trace Mercedes-Benz racing history, spanning more than a half-century.

valuable cars and components as early as 1923. This was expanded to include not just passenger cars and commercial vehicles, but racing cars, rail vehicles, and engines as well.

In 1936, Daimler-Benz paused to look back on 50 years of automobile manufacture and the first Daimler-Benz Museum was established to mark the occasion. For the first time, historical exhibits and the contemporary product range were displayed side by side.

During World War II, many valuable items had to be transferred to other quarters, and some were lost forever. Nevertheless, in the course of time, many of the most important vehicles were recovered and the collection was gradually rebuilt.

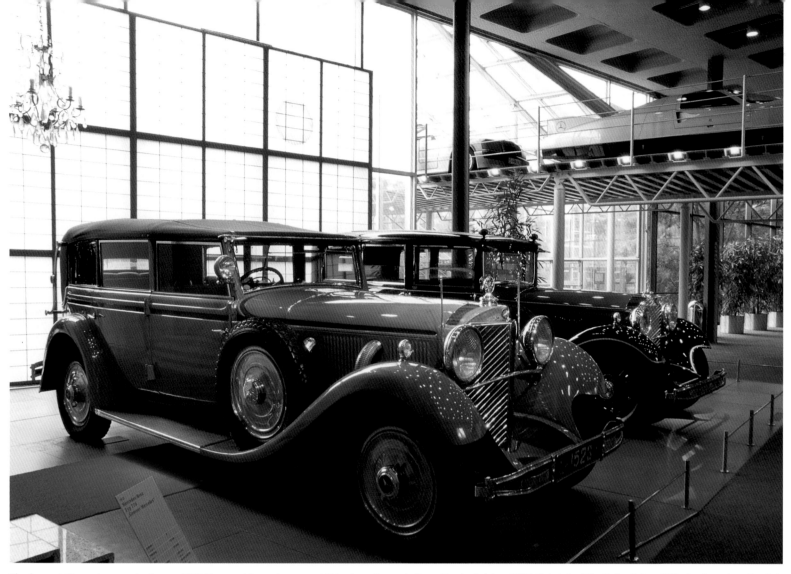

The largest Mercedes ever built, two 770 Grosser Mercedes are exhibited on the main floor. To the left is a 1931 Cabriolet F built for Kaiser Wilhelm II, and to the right is a 1935 770 Pullman Saloon produced for the Imperial Court of Japan.

In 1961, Daimler-Benz AG decided to erect a large new museum in Stuttgart-Untertürkheim, which received more than three million visitors before it closed for renovation and reorganization in 1985, in preparation for the 100th anniversary of the automobile in 1986.

In February 1986 the new Mercedes-Benz Museum opened its doors with a modern layout and a diversity of media that made individual exhibits come to life in their historical context. The open, naturally lighted architectural design of the museum and multistory spiral layout allows visitors to move about freely from one level to the next. The stunning glass ceilings permit the cars to be viewed in natural light, which, augmented by indirect illumination, allows every vehicle displayed to be seen in

A special exhibit just for the 540 K Special Roadster illustrates the importance of this model to Mercedes-Benz history.

187

On the top level of the museum, a special exhibit highlights the legendary 300 SL Coupe and Roadster in a neon-lighted display titled "The '50s."

Hard as it may be to believe, this streamlined W 125 Mercedes record car was designed in 1938! Rudolf Caracciola drove this car to a speed of 432.7 kilometers per hour (259.62 miles per hour) on a public road (closed for the speed run), a record that has never been broken.

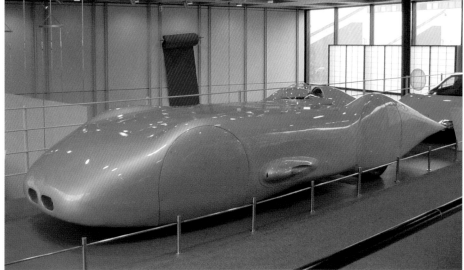

striking detail. The history of the company is also depicted in ground level displays that begin at the entrance with the 1886 Benz Patent Motorwagen and 1886 Daimler Motor Carriage and progress year by year through nearly a century of Mercedes, Benz, and Mercedes-Benz development.

Multimedia exhibits, including films and vintage racing footage, depict the historic achievements of the company on both road and track, and visitors can hear the history of the automobile in a variety of languages through the museum's cordless infrared Audio Information System, operating at every vehicle display.

The Mercedes-Benz Museum is more than just a collection of historical automobiles. It reflects the inventive talents, the striving for perfect solutions, the skillful craftsmanship and thoroughness on which the Mercedes-Benz tradition has been built for 115 years.

The museum is open Tuesday through Sunday from 9 AM to 5 PM except holidays. Admission is free.

For restorers and collectors from all over the world, the Mercedes-Benz Classic Center in nearby Fellbach is the fatherland, the source Mercedes. It is here that one might find, among other items, a brand-new 1928 Mercedes-Benz SSK cylinder head. Brand-new, as in new-old-stock? "Brand-new as in never out of the box," says Stefan Röhrig, senior manager of the Classic Center, where one can find just about anything ever built by Benz & Cie., Daimler-Motoren-Gesellschaft, and Daimler-Benz AG since 1900.

The Classic Center facility, distinguished by the striking black and white image of a Mercedes-Benz SSK

then a regal 1934 Type 200 Limousine. You can see them all, and if the spirit moves you, and your letter of credit is sufficient, you can buy any one of them, except for the Fangio and Moss race cars, which are so historically tied to Daimler-Benz that they will likely never know another owner.

Under one roof, albeit a very large one, you have historic racing cars on display, restored Mercedes spanning more than 70 years for sale, and it is all open to the public without appointment.

For Mercedes-Benz aficionados, this is the ultimate candy store. "The Classic Center is very much like a new car dealership, dealing in sales and service," says Röhrig, "except every car here is a classic." The center also serves Mercedes-Benz dealerships worldwide in need of repair parts for vintage Mercedes. "The parts business is very important, especially for the older cars," notes Röhrig. "Older," in this instance, means cars that have better than a half-century behind them. "Parts for cars built in the 1960s and 1970s are still available at most Mercedes-Benz dealerships," he says. "Here we deal in somewhat more esoteric items, like the SSK cylinder head, for example."

Modern speed is represented by the 1997 CART Manufacturers' Championship race car.

The imposing two-story Classic Center building opened in May 1993. The complex houses a complete body shop, engine shop, restoration facility, parts warehouse, showroom, gift shop, and gallery of historic Mercedes-Benz photographs. It's one-stop shopping, whether you want a post card of a 300 SL or the real thing.

painted across the face of a two-story-high building, is home to the world's finest collection of Mercedes-Benz parts and a restoration shop second to none. (The SSK has its exhaust pipes on the wrong side of the hood, because the image would not have worked facing the opposite direction due to a very old tree. In Green Germany, one does not remove the tree, one moves the exhaust pipes!) It is the shop Daimler-Benz entrusts with its very history. In the service bays and store rooms can be found race cars driven by Fangio and Moss, the 300 SLR of legendary chief engineer Rudolf Uhlenhaut, and every style of Mercedes-Benz motorcar, from antiques and classics, to the contemporary racing machines that have seared the silver star image into the winner's circles of every major racing venue around the world.

When one enters the Classic Center, the 115-year history of Mercedes-Benz dazzles the senses with monumental images of legendary cars lining the walls, shelves of books on Mercedes-Benz automobiles, and a first glance into a pristine showroom lined with cars that make your breath catch. "Isn't that an SSK? That . . . that's the car Stirling Moss drove in the 1955 Mille Miglia! You can see it. Touch it. There's a 300 SL in one row, a 600 Pullman in the next, a 300 S Coupe,

Juan Fangio's W 154 (Number 2) which he drove in Argentina in 1951. The W 154 was first raced in 1938. Following World War II, it was refurbished and campaigned by Fangio, in an impressive demonstration that a prewar car more than a dozen years old could still be competitive. The car was restored at the Classic Center.

Cars from all over the world arrive at the Classic Center for repair or restoration. After hours, the main floor of the Classic Center is a resting place for some of the marque's greatest cars, which occasionally spend a few needed weeks or months being partially or completely restored for their owners.

Looking over the main floor of the restoration facility from the second story balcony, Röhrig views the cars below and, drawing his lips tightly, states in an almost reverent voice, "We are responsible for 100 years of Daimler-Benz history. It is a very important role."

That role began in May 1993 when Daimler-Benz AG became the world's first automotive brand to set up its own classic car center. "By responding to the wishes of Mercedes owners and enthusiasts in this way, the company was effectively extending its role as guardian of the Mercedes tradition and at the same time providing an extra boost to the market in vintage Mercedes," observes Max-Gerrit von Pein, head of Daimler-Chrysler Classic. "I see the Classic Center as an ideal way of encouraging the public to develop and maintain an interest in the Mercedes tradition."

Within a few weeks of the center's opening, more than 600 inquiries a month were flooding in from all parts of the world. Since then, the number has risen to more than 2,000 per month, says Röhrig, figures that present ample testimony to the fact that Mercedes-Benz automobiles still enjoy worldwide popularity. The realization that so many older Mercedes are still on the road, are being campaigned in vintage racing, and are making the 1,000-mile trek in Americanized Mille Miglia tours from New England to Colorado, Arizona, and California not only demonstrates the longevity of Mercedes-Benz automobiles but the unquestionable need for the Classic Center to provide the rare and often impossible-to-locate parts that keep these motoring masterpieces on the road.

The Classic Center stocks more than 25,000 line items and procures another 15,000 rare and out of production parts from over 150 different suppliers around the world. "Whenever a part is ordered through the Classic Center," says Röhrig, "that part is thoroughly checked here before it is shipped. If a part is coming via the Classic Center, it is a Mercedes part."

The massive facility and its hand-selected staff service more than 1,000 cars each year, and of those 10 to 15 are there for partial or complete restorations. For Daimler-Benz, one entire department is dedicated solely to the restoration and maintaining of Mercedes-Benz racing cars. It is here within this wing, behind the showroom doors, that Daimler-Benz history permeates every square inch of floor space. "All of our race cars go through that workshop before going to an event," says Röhrig, standing alongside a W 196 once driven by Stirling Moss, and only yards from the 300 SLR Moss steered to victory in the 1955 Mille Miglia. These are priceless cars, valuable far beyond their material worth. They are history in the flesh.

"The main idea at the start was to improve the availability of spare parts for classic Mercedes-Benz models, and we have been highly successful in doing so," Röhrig says. "We have developed a real partnership not just with our customers, but with our parts suppliers around the world. And everyone has benefited." Between the parts resources and restoration facility, Mercedes-Benz owners the world over can now profit from the company's commitment to preserving its heritage.

The slogan around the Classic Center, "You can't get more original than this," really underscores the historic impact of this remarkable facility. When a car leaves the Fellbach restoration shop, it has been rebuilt by the original maker, and that's a statement no other restorer can make!

END NOTES

Chapter 1

[1] When Steinway died in 1896, the company was reorganized as Daimler Manufacturing Company of Long Island City. The company continued to produce engines, a line of motor launches, and a few commercial vehicles and to import Daimler automobiles. With the advent of the Mercedes, the Steinway Company decided to get into vehicle manufacturing. In 1905 it began producing the American Mercedes, an exact duplicate of the 45-horsepower model, which had become the rage of Europe. A disastrous fire razed the entire Long Island City factory in February 1907, bringing an end to the American-made Mercedes.

[2] Panhard & Levassor produced a similarly styled front-engine model in the early 1890s, powered by Daimler engines.

Chapter 2

[1] *The Star and the Laurel*, pg. 83.

[2] *The Star and the Laurel*, pg. 94.

Chapter 3

[1] *The Star and the Laurel* p. 137.

Chapter 4

[1] German specification indicated 80 horsepower while foreign sales literature claimed an output of 90 horsepower for the 460.

Chapter 6

[1] As noted by Daimler-Benz archives on the specifications for the 1952 prototype coupe.

Chapter 8

[1] *Mercedes-Benz Illustrated Buyer's Guide* by Frank Barrett, page 115.

[2] The 4-Matic System was available in Europe on 1986 and later sedans and station wagons, but not in the United States until the 1990 model year, when the first 4-Matic sedans and station wagons were offered. They were available through 1993 and discontinued until the new 4-Matic all-wheel-drive system was introduced in 1998.

[3] The 190 series in Germany included the 190 D diesel sedan, which was principally the model of choice for taxi work. Later models were 190 D 2.5 turbo.

Chapter 10

[1] Technically, it would be 100 years under the Mercedes name as the silver star was not adopted until 1909.

[2] *Mercedes-Benz Quicksilver Century* by Karl Ludvigsen, Transport Bookman Publications, Middlesex, England, 1995.

[3] Caracciola was driving for Alfa Romeo in 1932 and 1933 because Daimler-Benz did not pursue race activities these years. Manfred von Brauchitsch was racing as a privateer.

LEFT:
X-ray vision is not required at the Classic Center, which has one of the C-Class competition cars that campaigned in the 1996 European Touring Car Championship. The remarkably realistic graphic depicts everything beneath the hood. This car makes everyone do a double take, because you can't tell where the hood ends and the graphic begins!

Index